How to Succeed

By

Orison Swett Marden

HOW TO SUCCEED

CHAPTER I

FIRST, BE A MAN

The great need at this hour is manly men. We want no goody-goody piety; we have too much of it. We want men who will do right, though the heavens fall, who believe in God, and who will confess Him.—REV. W. J. DAWSON.

All the world cries, where is the man who will save us? We want a man! Don't look so far for this man. You have him at hand. This man—it is you, it is I; it is each one of us! How to constitute one's self a man? Nothing harder, if one knows not how to will it; nothing easier, if one wills it.—ALEXANDER DUMAS.

"I thank God I am a Baptist," said a little, short Doctor of Divinity, as he mounted a step at a convention. "Louder! louder!" shouted a man in the audience; "we can't hear." "Get up higher," said another. "I can't," replied the doctor, "to be a Baptist is as high as one can get."

But there is something higher than being a Baptist, and that is being a *man.*

Rousseau says: "According to the order of nature, men being equal, their common vocation is the profession of humanity; and whoever is well educated to discharge the duty of a man cannot be badly prepared to fill any of those offices that have a relation to him. It matters little to me whether my pupil be designed for the army, the pulpit, or the bar. To live is the profession I would teach him. When I have done with him, it is true he will be neither a soldier, a lawyer, nor a divine. *Let him first be a man;* Fortune may remove him from one rank to another, as she pleases, he will be always found in his place."

"First of all," replied the boy James A. Garfield, when asked what he meant to be, "I must make myself a man; if I do not succeed in that, I can succeed in nothing."

"Hear me, O men," cried Diogenes, in the market place at Athens; and, when a crowd collected around him, he said scornfully, "I called for men, not pigmies."

One great need of the world to-day is for men and women who are good animals. To endure the strain of our concentrated civilization, the coming man and woman must have an excess of animal spirits. They must have a robustness of health. Mere absence of disease is not health. It is the overflowing fountain, not the one half full that gives life and beauty to the valley below. Only he is healthy who exults in mere animal existence; whose very life is a luxury; who feels a bounding pulse throughout his body; who feels life in every limb, as dogs do when scouring over the field, or as boys do when gliding over fields of ice.

Dispense with the doctor by being temperate; the lawyer by keeping out of debt; the demagogue, by voting for honest men; and poverty, by being industrious.

"Nephew," said Sir Godfrey Kneller, the artist, to a Guinea slave trader, who entered the room where his uncle was talking with Alexander Pope, "you have the honor of seeing the two greatest men in the world." "I don't know how great men you may be," said the Guinea man, as he looked contemptuously upon their diminutive physical proportions, "but I don't like your looks; I have often bought a much better man than either of you, all muscles and bones, for ten guineas."

A man is never so happy as when he suffices to himself, and can walk without crutches or a guide. Said Jean Paul Richter: "I have made as much out of myself as could be made of the stuff, and no man should require more."

"The body of an athlete and the soul of a sage," wrote Voltaire to Helvetius; "these are what we require to be happy."

Although millions are out of employment in the United States, how difficult it is to find a thorough, reliable, self-dependent, industrious man or woman, young or old, for any position, whether as a domestic servant, an office boy, a teacher, a brakeman, a conductor, an engineer, a clerk, a bookkeeper, or whatever we may want. It is almost impossible to find a really *competent* person in any department, and oftentimes we have to make many trials before we can get a position fairly well filled.

It is a superficial age; very few prepare for their work. Of thousands of young women trying to get a living at typewriting, many are so ignorant, so deficient in the common rudiments even, that they spell badly, use bad grammar, and know scarcely anything of punctuation. In fact, they murder the English language. They can copy, "parrot like," and that is about all.

The same superficiality is found in nearly all kinds of business. It is next to impossible to get a first-class mechanic; he has not learned his trade; he has picked it up, and botches everything he touches, spoiling good material and wasting valuable time.

In the professions, it is true, we find greater skill and faithfulness, but usually they have been developed at the expense of mental and moral breadth.

The merely professional man is narrow; worse than that, he is in a sense an artificial man, a creature of technicalities and specialties, removed alike from the broad truth of nature and from the healthy influence of human converse. In society, the most accomplished man of mere professional skill is often a nullity; he has sunk his personality in his dexterity.

"The aim of every man," said Humboldt, "should be to secure the highest and most harmonious development of his powers to a complete and consistent whole."

Some men impress us as immense possibilities. They seem to have a sweep of intellect that is grand; a penetrative power that is phenomenal; they seem to know everything, to have read everything, to have seen everything. Nothing seems to escape the keenness of their vision. But somehow they are forever disappointing our expectations. They raise great hopes only to dash them. They are men of great promise, but they never pay. There is some indefinable want in their make-up.

What the world needs is a clergyman who is broader than his pulpit, who does not look upon humanity with a white neck cloth ideal, and who would give the lie to the saying that the human race is divided into three classes: men, women and ministers. Wanted, a clergyman who does not look upon his congregation from the standpoint of old theological books, and dusty, cobweb creeds, but who sees the merchant as in his store, the clerk as making sales, the lawyer pleading before the jury, the physician standing over the sick bed; in other words, who looks upon the great throbbing, stirring, pulsing, competing, scheming, ambitious, impulsive, tempted, mass of humanity as one of their number, who can live with them, see with their eyes, hear with their ears, and experience their sensations.

The world has a standing advertisement over the door of every profession, every occupation, every calling: "Wanted—A Man."

Wanted, a lawyer, who has not become the victim of his specialty, a mere walking bundle of precedents.

Wanted, a shopkeeper who does not discuss markets wherever he goes. A man should be so much larger than his calling, so broad and symmetrical in his culture, that he would not talk shop in society, that no one would suspect how he gets his living.

Nothing is more apparent in this age of specialties than the dwarfing, crippling, mutilating influence of occupations or professions. Specialties facilitate commerce, and promote efficiency in the professions, but are often narrowing to individuals. The spirit of the age tends to doom the lawyer to a narrow life of practice, the business man to a mere money-making career.

Think of a man, the grandest of God's creations, spending his life-time standing beside a machine for making screws. There is nothing to call out his individuality, his ingenuity, his powers of balancing, judging, and deciding.

He stands there year after year, until he seems but a piece of mechanism. His powers, from lack of use, dwindle to mediocrity, to inferiority, until finally he becomes a mere part of the machine he tends.

Wanted, a man who will not lose his individuality in a crowd, a man who has the courage of his convictions, who is not afraid to say "No," though all the world say "Yes."

Wanted, a man who, though he is dominated by a mighty purpose, will not permit one great faculty to dwarf, cripple, warp, or mutilate his manhood; who will not allow the over-development of one faculty to stunt or paralyze his other faculties.

Wanted, a man who is larger than his calling, who considers it a low estimate of his occupation to value it merely as a means of getting a living. Wanted, a man who sees self-development, education and culture, discipline and drill, character and manhood, in his occupation.

As Nature tries every way to induce us to obey her laws by rewarding their observance with health, pleasure and happiness, and punishes their violation by pain and disease, so she resorts to every means to induce us to expand and develop the great possibilities she has implanted within us. She nerves us to the struggle, beneath which all great blessings are buried, and beguiles the tedious marches by holding up before us glittering prizes, which we may almost touch, but never quite possess. She covers up her ends of discipline by trial, of character building through suffering by throwing a splendor and glamour over the future; lest the hard, dry facts of the present dishearten us, and she fail in her great purpose. How else could Nature call the youth away from all the charms that hang around young life, but by presenting to his imagination pictures of future bliss and greatness which will haunt his dreams until he resolves to make them real. As a mother teaches her babe to walk, by holding up a toy at a distance, not that the child may reach the toy, but that it may develop its muscles and strength, compared with which the toys are mere baubles; so Nature goes before us through life, tempting us with higher and higher toys, but ever with one object in view—the development of the man.

In every great painting of the masters there is one idea or figure which stands out boldly beyond everything else. Every other idea or figure on the canvas is subordinate to this idea or figure, and finds its real significance not in itself, but, pointing to the central idea, finds its true expression there. So in the vast universe of God, every object of creation is but a guide-board with an index finger pointing to the central figure of the created universe—Man. Nature writes this thought upon every leaf; she thunders it in every creation; it exhales from every flower; it twinkles in every star.

Open thy bosom, set thy wishes wide, And let in manhood—let in happiness;
Admit the boundless theatre of thought From nothing up to God ... which
makes a man!—YOUNG.

CHAPTER II

SEIZE YOUR OPPORTUNITY

"The blowing winds are but our servants When we hoist a sail."

You must come to know that each admirable genius is but a successful diver in that sea whose floor of pearls is all your own.—EMERSON.

Who waits until the wind shall silent keep, Who never finds the ready hour to sow, Who watcheth clouds, will have no time to reap.—HELEN HUNT JACKSON.

The secret of success in life is for a man *to be ready for his opportunity* when it comes.—DISRAELI.

Do the best you can where you are; and, when that is accomplished, God will open a door for you, and a voice will call, "Come up hither into a higher sphere."—BEECHER.

Our grand business is, not to see what lies dimly at a distance, but to do what lies clearly at hand.—CARLYLE.

"When I was a boy," said General Grant, "my mother one morning found herself without butter for breakfast, and sent me to borrow some from a neighbor. Going into the house without knocking, I overheard a letter read from the son of a neighbor, who was then at West Point, stating that he had failed in examination and was coming home. I got the butter, took it home, and, without waiting for breakfast ran to the office of the congressman for our district. 'Mr. Hamer,' I said, 'will you appoint me to West Point?' 'No, —— is there, and has three years to serve.' 'But suppose he should fail, will you send me?' Mr. Hamer laughed. 'If he don't go through, no use for you to try, Uly.' 'Promise me you will give me the chance, Mr. Hamer, anyhow.' Mr. Hamer promised. The next day the defeated lad came home, and the congressman, laughing at my sharpness, gave me the appointment. Now," said Grant, "it was my mother's being without butter that made me general and president." But he was mistaken. It was his own shrewdness to see the chance, and the promptness to seize it, that urged him upward.

"There is nobody," says a Roman Cardinal, "whom Fortune does not visit once in his life; but when she finds he is not ready to receive her, she goes in at the door, and out through the window." Opportunity is coy. The careless, the slow, the unobservant, the lazy fail to see it, or clutch at it when it has gone. The sharp fellows detect it instantly, and catch it when on the wing.

The utmost which can be said about the matter is, that circumstances will, and do combine to help men at some periods of their lives, and combine to thwart them at others. Thus much we freely admit; but there is no fatality in these combinations, neither any such thing as "luck" or "chance," as commonly understood. They come and go like all other opportunities and occasions in life, and if they are seized upon and made the most of, the man whom they benefit is fortunate; but if they are neglected and allowed to pass by unimproved, he is unfortunate.

"Charley," says Moses H. Grinnell to a clerk born in New York City, "take my overcoat tip to my house on Fifth Avenue." Mr. Charley takes the coat, mutters something about "I'm not an errand boy. I came here to learn business," and moves reluctantly. Mr. Grinnell sees it, and at the same time one of his New England clerks says, "I'll take it up." "That is right, do so," says Mr. G., and to himself he says, "that boy is smart, he will work," and he gives him plenty to do. He gets promoted, gets the confidence of business men as well as of his employers, and is soon known as a successful man.

The youth who starts out in life determined to make the most of his eyes and let nothing escape him which he can possibly use for his own advancement, who keeps his ears open for every sound that can help him on his way, who keeps his hands open that he may clutch every opportunity, who is ever on the alert for everything which can help him to get on in the world, who seizes every experience in life and grinds it up into paint for his great life's picture, who keeps his heart open that he may catch every noble impulse and everything which may inspire him, will be sure to live a successful life; there are no ifs or ands about it. If he has his health, nothing can keep him from success.

Zion's Herald says that Isaac Rich, who gave one million and three quarters to found Boston University of the Methodist Episcopal Church, began business thus: at eighteen he went from Cape Cod to Boston with three or four dollars in his possession, and looked about for something to do, rising early, walking far, observing closely, reflecting much. Soon he had an idea: he bought three bushels of oysters, hired a wheelbarrow, found a piece of board, bought six small plates, six iron forks, a three-cent pepper-box, and one or two other things. He was at the oyster-boat buying his oysters at three o'clock in the morning, wheeled them three miles, set up his board near a market, and began business. He sold out his oysters as fast as he could get them, at a good profit. In that same market he continued to deal in oysters and fish for forty years, became king of the business, and ended by founding a college. His success was won by industry and honesty.

"Give me a chance," says Haliburton's Stupid, "and I will show you." But most likely he has had his chance already and neglected it.

"Well, boys," said Mr. A., a New York merchant, to his four clerks one winter morning in 1815, "this is good news. Peace has been declared. Now *we* must be up and doing. We shall have our hands full, but we can do as much as anybody."

He was owner and part owner of several ships lying dismantled during the war, three miles up the river, which was covered with ice an inch thick. He knew that it would be a month before the ice yielded for the season, and that thus the merchants in other towns where the harbors were open, would have time to be in the foreign markets before him. His decision therefore was instantly taken.

"Reuben," he continued, addressing one of his clerks, "go and collect as many laborers as possible to go up the river. Charles, do you find Mr.——, the rigger, and Mr.——, the sailmaker, and tell them I want them immediately. John, engage half-a-dozen truckmen for to-day and to-morrow. Stephen, do you hunt up as many gravers and caulkers as you can, and hire them to work for me." And Mr. A. himself sallied forth to provide the necessary implements for icebreaking. Before twelve o'clock that day, upward of an hundred men were three miles up the river, clearing the ships and cutting away ice, which they sawed out in large squares, and then thrust under the main mass to open up the channel. The roofing over the ships was torn off, and the clatter of the caulkers' mallets was like to the rattling of a hail-storm, loads of rigging were passed up on the ice, riggers went to and fro with belt and knife, sailmakers busily plied their needles, and the whole presented an unusual scene of stir and activity and well-directed labor. Before night the ships were afloat, and moved some distance down the channel; and by the time they had reached the wharf, namely, in some eight or ten days, their rigging and spars were aloft, their upper timbers caulked, and everything ready for them to go to sea.

Thus Mr. A. competed on equal terms with the merchants of open seaports. Large and quick gains rewarded his enterprise, and then his neighbors spoke depreciatingly of his "good luck." But, as the writer from whom we get the story says, Mr. A. was equal to his opportunity, and this was the secret of his good fortune.

A Baltimore lady lost a valuable diamond bracelet at a ball, and supposed it was stolen from the pocket of her cloak. Years afterward, she walked the streets near the Peabody Institute to get money to purchase food. She cut up an old, worn out, ragged cloak to make a hood of, when lo! in the lining of the cloak, she discovered the diamond bracelet. During all her poverty she was worth thirty-five hundred dollars, but did not know it.

Many of us who think we are poor are rich in opportunities if we could only see them, in possibilities all about us, in faculties worth more than diamond bracelets, in power to do good.

In our large eastern cities it has been found that at least ninety-four out of every hundred found their first fortune at home, or near at hand, and in meeting common everyday wants. It is a sorry day for a young man who cannot see any opportunities where he is, but thinks he can do better somewhere else.

Several Brazilian shepherds organized a party to go to California to dig gold, and took along a handful of clear pebbles to play checkers with on the voyage. They discovered after arriving at Sacramento, after they had thrown most of the pebbles away, that they were all diamonds. They returned to Brazil only to find that the mines had been taken up by others and sold to the government.

The richest gold and silver mine in Nevada was sold for forty-two dollars by the owner, to get money to pay his passage to other mines where he thought he could get rich.

Professor Agassiz told the Harvard students of a farmer who owned a farm of hundreds of acres of unprofitable woods and rocks, and concluded to sell out and try some more remunerative business.

He studied coal measures and coal oil deposits, and experimented for a long time. He sold his farm for two hundred dollars and went into the oil business two hundred miles away. Only a short time afterward the man who bought the farm discovered a great flood of coal oil, which the farmer had ignorantly tried to drain off.

A man was once sitting in an uncomfortable chair in Boston talking with a friend as to what he could do to help mankind. "I should think it would be a good thing," said the friend, "to begin by getting up an easier and cheaper chair."

"I will do it," he exclaimed, leaping up and examining the chair. He found a great deal of rattan thrown away by the East India merchant ships, whose cargoes were wrapped in it. He began the manufacture of rattan chairs and other furniture, and has astonished the world by what he has done with what was before thrown away. While this man was dreaming about some far off success, he at that very time had fortune awaiting only his ingenuity and industry.

If you want to get rich, study yourself and your own wants. You will find millions of others have the same wants, the same demands. The safest business is always connected with men's prime necessities. They must have clothing, dwellings; they must eat. They want comforts, facilities of all kinds, for use and pleasure, luxury, education, culture. Any man who can supply a great want of humanity, improve any methods which men use, supply any demand or contribute in any way to their well-being, can make a fortune.

But it is detrimental to the highest success to undertake anything merely because it is profitable. If the vocation does not supply a human want, if it is not healthful, if it is degrading, if it is narrowing, don't touch it.

A selfish vocation never pays. If it belittles the manhood, blights the affections, dwarfs the mental life, chills the charities and shrivels the soul, don't touch it. Choose that occupation, if possible, which will be the most helpful to the largest number.

It is estimated that five out of every seven of the millionaire manufacturers began by making with their own hands the articles on which they made their fortune.

One of the greatest hindrances to advancement and promotion in life is the lack of observation and the disinclination to take pains. A keen, cultivated observation will see a fortune where others see only poverty. An observing man, the eyelets of whose shoes pulled out, but who could ill afford to get another pair, said to himself, "I will make a metallic lacing hook, which can be riveted into the leather." He succeeded in doing so and now he is a very rich man.

An observing barber in Newark, N. J., thought he could make an improvement on shears for cutting hair, and invented "clippers" and became very rich. A Maine man was called from the hayfield to wash out the clothes for his invalid wife. He had never realized what it was to wash before. He invented the washing-machine and made a fortune. A man who was suffering terribly with toothache, said to himself, "There must be some way of filling teeth to prevent them aching;" he invented gold filling for teeth.

The great things of the world have not been done by men of large means. Want has been the great schoolmaster of the race: necessity has been the mother of all great inventions. Ericsson began the construction of a screw-propeller in a bath-room. John Harrison, the great inventor of the marine chronometer, began his career in the loft of an old barn. Parts of the first steamboat ever run in America were set up in the vestry of an old church in Philadelphia by Fitch. McCormick began to make his famous reaper in an old grist-mill. The first model dry-dock was made in an attic. Clark, the founder of Clark University of Worcester, Mass., began his great fortune by making toy wagons in a horse-shed.

Opportunities? They crowd around us. Forces of nature plead to be used in the service of man, as lightning for ages tried to attract his attention to electricity, which would do his drudgery and leave him to develop the God-given powers within him.

There is power lying latent everywhere, waiting for the observant eye to discover it.

First find out what the people need and then supply that want. An invention to make the smoke go the wrong way in a chimney might be a very ingenious thing, but it would be of no use to humanity. The patent office at Washington is full of wonderful devices, ingenious mechanism; not one in hundreds is of earthly use to the inventor or to the world, and yet how many families have been impoverished and have struggled for years mid want and woe, while the father has been working on useless inventions. These men did not study the wants of humanity. A. T. Stewart, as a boy, lost eighty-seven cents when his capital was one dollar and a half, in buying buttons and thread which people would not purchase. After that he made it a rule never to buy anything which people did not want.

The first thing a youth, entering the city to make his home there, needs to do is to make himself a necessity to the person who employs him, according to the Boston *Herald*. Whatever he may have been at home, it counts for nothing until he has done something that makes known the quality of the stuff that is in him. If he shirks work, however humble it may be, the work will soon be inclined to shirk him. But the youth who comes into a city to make his way in the world, and is not afraid of doing his best whether he is paid for it or not, is not long in finding remunerative employment. The people who seem so indifferent to employing young people from the country are eagerly watching for the newcomers, but they look for qualities of character and service in actual work before they manifest confidence or give recognition. It is the youth who is deserving that wins his way to the front, and when once he has been tested his promotion is only a question of time. It is the same with young women. There are seemingly no places for them where they can earn a decent living, but the moment they fill their places worthily there is room enough for them, and progress is rapid. What the city people desire most is to find those who have ability to take important places, and the question of gaining a position in the city resolves itself at once into the question of what the young persons have brought with them from home. It is the staying qualities that have been in-wrought from childhood which are now in requisition, and the success of the boy or girl is determined by the amount of energetic character that has been developed in the early years at home. Take up the experience of every man or woman who has made a mark in the city for the last hundred years, and it has been the sterling qualities of the home training that have constituted the success of later years.

Don't think you have no chance in life because you have no capital to begin with. Most of the rich men of to-day began poor. The chances are you would be ruined if you had capital. You can only use to advantage what has become a part of yourself by your earning it. It is estimated that not one rich man's son in ten thousand dies rich. God has given every man a capital to start with; we are born rich. He is rich who has good health, a sound body, good muscles; he is rich who has a good head, a good disposition, a good heart; he is rich who has two good hands, with five chances on each. Equipped? Every man is equipped as only God could equip him. What a fortune he possesses in the marvelous mechanism of his body and mind. It is individual effort that has accomplished everything worth accomplishing in this world. Money to start with is only a crutch, which, if any misfortune knocks it from under you, would only make your fall all the more certain.

CHAPTER III

HOW DID HE BEGIN?

There can be no doubt that the captains of industry to-day, using that term in its broadest sense, are men who began life as poor boys.—SETH LOW.

Poverty is very terrible, and sometimes kills the very soul within us, but it is the north wind that lashes men into Vikings; it is the soft, luscious south wind which lulls them to lotus dreams.—OUIDA.

'Tis a common proof,That lowliness is young ambition's ladder—SHAKESPEARE.

"Fifty years ago," said Hezekiah Conant, the millionaire manufacturer and philanthropist of Pawtucket, R. I., "I persuaded my father to let me leave my home in Dudley, Mass., and strike out for myself. So one morning in May, 1845, the old farm horse and wagon was hitched up, and, dressed in our Sunday clothes, father and I started for Worcester. Our object was to get me the situation offered by an advertisement in the Worcester County *Gazette* as follows:

BOY WANTED.

WANTED IMMEDIATELY.—At the *Gazette* Office, a well disposed boy, able to do heavy rolling. Worcester, May 7.

"The financial inducements were thirty dollars the first year, thirty-five the next, and forty dollars the third year and board in the employer's family. These conditions were accepted, and I began work the next day. The *Gazette* was an ordinary four-page sheet. I soon learned what 'heavy rolling' meant for the paper was printed on a 'Washington' hand-press, the edition of about 2000 copies requiring two laborious intervals of about ten hours each, every week. The printing of the outside was generally done Friday and kept me very busy all day. The inside went to press about three or four o'clock Tuesday afternoon, and it was after three o'clock on Wednesday morning before I could go to bed, tired and lame from the heavy rolling. In addition, I also had the laborious task of carrying a quantity of water from the pump behind the block around to the entrance in front, and then up two flights of stairs, usually a daily job. I was at first everybody's servant. I was abused, called all sorts of nicknames, had to sweep out the office, build fires in winter, run errands, post bills, carry papers, wait on the editor, in fact I led the life of a genuine printer's devil; but when I showed them at length that I had learned to set type and run the press, I got promoted, and another boy was hired to succeed to my task, with all its decorations. That was my first success, and from that day to this I have never asked anybody to get me a job or situation, and never used a letter of recommendation; but when an important job was in prospect the proposed employers were given all facilities to learn of my abilities and character. If some young men are easily discouraged, I hope they may gain encouragement and strength from my story. It is a long, rough road at first, but, like the ship on the ocean, you must lay your course for the place where you hope to land, and take advantage of all favoring circumstances."

"Don't go about the town any longer in that outlandish rig. Let me give you an order on the store. Dress up a little, Horace." Horace Greeley looked down on his clothes as if he had never before noticed how seedy they were, and replied: "You see, Mr. Sterrett, my father is on a new place, and I want to help him all I can." He had spent but six dollars for personal expenses in seven months, and was to receive one hundred and thirty-five from Judge J. M. Sterrett of the Erie *Gazette* for substitute work. He retained but fifteen dollars and gave the rest to his father, with whom he had moved from Vermont to Western Pennsylvania, and for whom he had camped out many a night to guard the sheep from wolves. He was nearly twenty-one; and, although tall and gawky, with tow-colored hair, a pale face and whining voice, he resolved to seek his fortune in New York City. Slinging his bundle of clothes on a stick over his shoulder, he walked sixty miles through the woods to Buffalo, rode on a canal boat to Albany, descended the Hudson in a barge, and reached New York, just as the sun was rising, August 18, 1831.

For days Horace wandered up and down the streets, going into scores of buildings and asking if they wanted "a hand;" but "no" was the invariable reply. His quaint appearance led many to think he was an escaped apprentice. One Sunday at his boarding-place he heard that printers were wanted at "West's Printing-office." He was at the door at five o'clock Monday morning, and asked the foreman for a job at seven. The latter had no idea that the country greenhorn could set type for the Polyglot Testament on which help was needed, but said: "Fix up a case for him and we'll see if he *can* do anything." When the proprietor came in, he objected to the newcomer and told the foreman to let him go when his first day's work was done. That night Horace showed a proof of the largest and most correct day's work that had then been done. In ten years Horace was a partner in a small printing-office. He founded the *New Yorker*, the best weekly paper in the United States, but it was not profitable. When Harrison was nominated for President in 1840, Greeley started *The Log Cabin*, which reached the then fabulous circulation of ninety thousand. But on this paper at a penny a copy, he made no money. His next venture was the New York *Tribune*, price one cent. To start it he borrowed a thousand dollars and printed five thousand copies of the first number. It was difficult to give them all away. He began with six hundred subscribers, and increased the list to eleven thousand in six weeks. The demand for the *Tribune* grew faster than new machinery could be obtained to print it. It was a paper whose editor always tried to be *right*.

At the World's Fair in New York in 1853 President Pierce might have been seen watching a young man exhibiting a patent rat trap. He was attracted by the enthusiasm and diligence of the young man, but never dreamed that he would become one of the richest men in the world. It seemed like small business for Jay Gould to be exhibiting a rat trap, but he did it well and with enthusiasm. In fact he was bound to do it as well as it could be done. Young Gould supported himself by odd jobs at surveying, paying his way by erecting sundials for farmers at a dollar apiece, frequently taking his pay in board. Thus he laid the foundation for the business career in which he became so rich.

Fred. Douglass started in life with less than nothing, for he did not own his own body, and he was pledged before his birth to pay his master's debts. To reach the starting-point of the poorest white boy, he had to climb as far as the distance which the latter must ascend if he would become President of the United States. He saw his mother but two or three times, and then in the night, when she would walk twelve miles to be with him an hour, returning in time to go into the field at dawn. He had no chance to study, for he had no teacher, and the rules of the plantation forbade slaves to learn to read and write. But somehow, unnoticed by his master, he managed to learn the alphabet from scraps of paper and patent medicine almanacs, and no limits could then be placed to his career. He put to shame thousands of white boys. He fled from slavery at twenty-one, went North and worked as a stevedore in New York and New Bedford. At Nantucket he was given an opportunity to speak in an anti-slavery meeting, and made so favorable an impression that he was made agent of the Anti-Slavery Society of Massachusetts. While traveling from place to place to lecture, he would study with all his might. He was sent to Europe to lecture, and won the friendship of several Englishmen, who gave him $750, with which he purchased his freedom. He edited a paper in Rochester, N. Y., and afterward con ducted the *New Era* in Washington. For several years he was Marshal of the District of Columbia. He became the first colored man in the United States, the peer of any man in the country, and died honored by all in 1895.

"What has been done can be done again," said the boy with no chance who became Lord Beaconsfield, England's great prime minister. "I am not a slave, I am not a captive, and by energy I can overcome greater obstacles." Jewish blood flowed in his veins, and everything seemed against him, but he remembered the example of Joseph, who became prime minister of Egypt four thousand years before, and that of Daniel, who was prime minister to the greatest despot of the world five centuries before the birth of Christ. He pushed his way up through the lower classes, up through the middle classes, up through the upper classes, until he stood a master, self-poised upon the topmost round of political and social power. Rebuffed, scorned, ridiculed, hissed down in the House of Commons, he simply said, "The time will come when you shall hear me." The time did come, and the boy with no chance but a determined will, swayed the sceptre of England for a quarter of a century.

"I learned grammar when I was a private soldier on the pay of sixpence a day," said William Cobbett. "The edge of my berth, or that of the guard-bed, was my seat to study in; my knapsack was my bookcase; a bit of board lying on my lap was my writing table, and the task did not demand anything like a year of my life. I had no money to purchase candles or oil; in winter it was rarely that I could get any evening light but that of the fire, and only my turn, even of that. To buy a pen or a sheet of paper I was compelled to forego some portion of my food, though in a state of half starvation. I had no moment of time that I could call my own, and I had to read and write amidst the talking, laughing, singing, whistling, and bawling of at least half a score of the most thoughtless of men, and that, too, in the hours of their freedom from all control. Think not lightly of the *farthing* I had to give, now and then, for pen, ink, or paper. That farthing was, alas! a great sum to me. I was as tall as I am now, and I had great health and great exercise. The whole of the money not expended for us at market was *twopence a week* for each man. I remember, and well I may! that upon one occasion I had, after all absolutely necessary expenses, on a Friday, made shift to have a half-penny in reserve, which I had destined for the purchase of a red herring in the morning, but when I pulled off my clothes at night, so hungry then as to be hardly able to endure life, I found that I had lost my half-penny. I buried my head under the miserable sheet and rug, and cried like a child.

"If I, under such circumstances, could encounter and overcome this task," he added, "is there, can there be in the world, a youth to find any excuse for its non-performance?"

"I have talked with great men," Lincoln told his fellow-clerk and friend, Greene, according to *McClure's Magazine*, "and I do not see how they differ from others."

He made up his mind to put himself before the public, and talked of his plans to his friends. In order to keep in practice in speaking he walked seven or eight miles to debating clubs. "Practicing polemics," was what he called the exercise.

He seems now for the first time to have begun to study subjects. Grammar was what he chose. He sought Mentor Graham, the schoolmaster, and asked his advice.

"If you are going before the public," Mr. Graham told him, "you ought to do it."

But where could he get a grammar? There was but one in the neighborhood, Mr. Graham said, and that was six miles away.

Without waiting for more information the young man rose from the breakfast-table, walked immediately to the place, borrowed this rare copy of

Kirkham's Grammar, and before night was deep in its mysteries. From that time on for weeks he gave every moment of his leisure to mastering the contents of the book. Frequently he asked his friend Greene to "hold the book" while he recited, and when puzzled by a point he would consult Mr. Graham.

Lincoln's eagerness to learn was such that the whole neighborhood became interested. The Greenes lent him books, the schoolmaster kept him in mind and helped him as he could, and even the village cooper let him come into his shop and keep up a fire of shavings sufficiently bright to read by at night. It was not long before the grammar was mastered.

"Well," Lincoln said to his fellow-clerk, Greene, "if that's what they call science, I think I'll go at another."

He had made another discovery—that he could conquer subjects.

The poor and friendless lad, George Peabody, weary, footsore and hungry, called at a tavern in Concord, N. H., and asked to be allowed to saw wood for lodging and breakfast. Half a century later he called there again, but then George Peabody was one of the greatest millionaire bankers of the world. Bishop Fowler says: "It is one of the greatest encouragements of our age, that ordinary men with extraordinary industry reach the highest stations."

Greeley's father, because the boy tried to yoke the off ox on the near side, said: "Ah! that boy will never get along in the world. He'll never know enough to come in when it rains."

He was too poor to wear stockings. But Horace persevered, and became one of the greatest editors of his century.

Handel's father hated music, and would not allow a musical instrument in the house; but the boy with an aim secured a little spinet, hid it in the attic, where he practiced every minute he could steal without detection, until he surprised the great players and composers of Europe by his wonderful knowledge of music. He was very practical in his work, and studied the taste and sensitiveness of audiences until he knew exactly what they wanted; then he would compose something to supply the demand. He analyzed the effect of sounds and combinations of sounds upon the senses, and wrote directly to human needs. His greatest work, "The Messiah," was composed in Dublin for the benefit of poor debtors who were imprisoned there. The influence of this masterpiece was tremendous. It was said it out-preached the preacher, out-prayed prayers, reformed the wayward, softened stony hearts, as it told the wonderful story of redemption, in sound.

A. T. Stewart began life as a teacher in New York at $300 a year. He soon resigned and began that career as a merchant in which he achieved a success almost with out precedent. Honesty, one price, cash on delivery, and business on business principles were his invariable rules. Absolute regularity and system reigned in every department. In fifty years he made a fortune of from thirty to forty million dollars. He was nominated as Secretary of the Treasury in 1869, but it was found that the law forbids a merchant to occupy that position. He offered to resign, or to give the entire profits of his business to the poor of New York as long as he should remain in office. President Grant declined to accept such an offer.

Poor Kepler struggled with constant anxieties, and told fortunes by astrology for a livelihood, saying that astrology as the daughter of astronomy ought to keep her mother; but fancy a man of science wasting precious time over horoscopes. "I supplicate you," he writes to Moestlin, "if there is a situation vacant at Tübingen, do what you can to obtain it for me, and let me know the prices of bread and wine and other necessaries of life, for my wife is not accustomed to live on beans." He had to accept all sorts of jobs; he made almanacs, and served anyone who would pay him.

Who could have predicted that the modest, gentle boy, Raphael, without either riches or noted family, would have worked his way to such renown, or that one of his pictures, but sixty-six and three-quarter inches square (the Mother of Jesus), would be sold to the Empress of Russia, for $66,000? His Ansedei Madonna, was bought by the National Gallery for $350,000. Think of Michael Angelo working for six florins a month, and eighteen years on St. Peter's for nothing!

Dr. Johnson was so afflicted with king's-evil that he lost the use of one eye. The youth could not even engage in the pastimes of his mates, as he could not see the gutter without bending his head down near the street. He read and studied terribly. Finally a friend offered to send him to Oxford, but he failed to keep his promise, and the boy had to leave. He returned home, and soon afterward his father died insolvent. He conquered adverse fortune and bodily infirmities with the fortitude of a true hero.

Ichabod Washburn, a poor boy born near Plymouth Rock, was apprenticed to a blacksmith in Worcester, Mass., and was so bashful that he scarcely dared to eat in the presence of others; but he determined that he would make the best wire in the world, and would contrive ways and means to manufacture it in enormous quantities. At that time there was no good wire made in the United States. One house in England had the monopoly of making steel wire for pianos for more than a century. Young Washburn, however, had grit, and was bound to succeed. His wire became the standard everywhere. At one time he made 250,000 yards of iron wire daily, consuming twelve tons of metal, and requiring the services of seven hundred men. He amassed an immense fortune, of which he gave away a large part during his life, and bequeathed the balance to charitable institutions.

John Jacob Astor left home at seventeen to acquire a fortune. His capital consisted of two dollars, and three resolutions,—to be honest, to be industrious and not to gamble. Two years later he reached New York, and began work in a fur store at two dollars a week and his board. Soon learning the details of the business, he began operations on his own account. By giving personal attention to every purchase and sale, roaming the woods to trade with the Indians, or crossing the Atlantic to sell his furs at a great profit in England, he soon became the leading fur dealer in the United States. His idea of what constitutes a fortune expanded faster than his acquisitions. At fifty he owned millions; at sixty his millions owned him. He invested in land, becoming in time the richest owner of real estate in America. Generous to his family, he seldom gave much for charity. He once subscribed fifty dollars for some benevolent purpose, when one of the committee of solicitation said, "We did hope for more, Mr. Astor. Your son gave us a hundred dollars." "Ah!" chuckled the rich furrier, "William has a rich father. Mine was poor."

Elihu Burritt wrote in a diary kept at Worcester, whither he went to enjoy its library privileges, such entries as these: "Monday, June 18, headache, 40 pages Cuvier's 'Theory of the Earth,' 64 pages of French, 11 hours' forging. Tuesday, June 19, 60 lines Hebrew, 30 Danish, 10 lines Bohemian, 9 lines Polish, 15 names of stars, 10 hours' forging. Wednesday, June 20, 25 lines Hebrew, 8 lines Syriac, 11 hours' forging." He mastered eighteen languages and thirty-two dialects. He became eminent as the "Learned Blacksmith," and for his noble work in the service of humanity. Edward Everett said of the manner in which this boy with no chance acquired great learning: "It is enough to make one who has good opportunities for education hang his head in shame."

"I was born in poverty," said Vice-President Henry Wilson. "Want sat by my cradle. I know what it is to ask a mother for bread when she has none to give. I left my home at ten years of age, and served an apprenticeship of eleven years, receiving a month's schooling each year, and, at the end of eleven years of hard work, a yoke of oxen and six sheep, which brought me eighty-four dollars. I never spent the sum of one dollar for pleasure, counting every penny from the time I was born till I was twenty-one years of age. I know what it is to travel weary miles and ask my fellow-men to give me leave to toil. * * * In the first month after I was twenty-one years of age, I went into the woods, drove a team, and cut mill-logs. I rose in the morning before daylight and worked hard till after dark, and received the magnificent sum of six dollars for the month's work! Each of these dollars looked as large to me as the moon looks to-night."

"Many a farmer's son," says Thurlow Weed, "has found the best opportunities for mental improvement in his intervals of leisure while tending 'sap-bush.' Such, at any rate, was my own experience. At night you had only to feed the kettles and keep up the fires, the sap having been gathered and the wood cut before dark. During the day we would always lay in a good stock of 'fat-pine' by the light of which, blazing bright before the sugar-house, in the posture the serpent was condemned to assume, as a penalty for tempting our first grandmother, I passed many a delightful night in reading. I remember in this way to have read a history of the French Revolution, and to have obtained from it a better and more enduring knowledge of its events and horrors and of the actors in that great national tragedy, than I have received from all subsequent reading. I remember also how happy I was in being able to borrow the books of a Mr. Keyes after a two-mile tramp through the snow, shoeless, my feet swaddled in remnants of rag carpet."

"That fellow will beat us all some day," said a merchant, speaking of John Wanamaker and his close attention to his work. What a prediction to make of a young man who started business with a little clothing in a hand cart in the streets of Philadelphia. But this youth had *the indomitable spirit of a conqueror in him*, and you could not keep him down. General Grant said to George W. Childs, "Mr. Wanamaker could command an army." His great energy, method, industry, economy, and high moral principle, attracted President Harrison, who appointed him Postmaster-General.

Jacques Aristide Boucicault began his business life as an employé in a dry goods house in a small provincial town in France. After a few years he went to Paris, where he prospered so rapidly that in 1853 he became a partner and later the sole proprietor of the Bon Marché, then only a small shop, which became under his direction the most unique establishment in the world. His idea was to establish a combined philanthropic and commercial house on a large scale. Every one who worked for him was advanced progressively, according to his length of employment and the value of the services he rendered. He furnished free tuition, free medical attendance, and a free library for employés; a provident fund affording a small capital for males and a marriage portion for females at the expiration of ten or fifteen years of service; a free reading room for the public; and a free art gallery for artists to exhibit their paintings or sculptures. After his sudden death in 1877, his only son carried forward his father's projects until he, too, died in 1879, when his widow, Marguerite Guerin, continued and extended his business and beneficent plans until her death in 1887. So well did this family lay the foundations of a building covering 108,000 square feet, with many accessory buildings of smaller size, and of a business employing 3600 persons with sales amounting to nearly $20,000,000 annually, that every department is still conducted with all its former success in accordance with the instructions of the founders. They are here no longer in their bodily presence, but their spirit, their ideas, still pervade the vast establishment. Everything is still sold at a small profit and at a price plainly marked, and any article which may have ceased to please the purchaser can, without the slightest difficulty, be exchanged or its value refunded.

When James Gordon Bennett was forty years old, he collected all his property, three hundred dollars, and in a cellar with a board upon two barrels for a desk, himself his own type setter, office boy, publisher, newsboy, clerk, editor, proof-reader and printer's devil, he started the New York *Herald*. In all his literary work up to this time he had tried to imitate Franklin's style; and, as is the fate of all imitators, he utterly failed.

He lost twenty years of his life trying to be somebody else. He first showed the material he was made of in the "Salutatory," of the *Herald*, viz., "Our only guide shall be good, sound and practical common-sense applicable to the business and bosoms of men engaged in everyday life. We shall support no party, be the organ of no faction or coterie, and care nothing for any election or any candidate from President down to constable. We shall endeavor to record facts upon every public and proper subject stripped of verbiage and coloring, with comments when suitable, just, independent, fearless and good-tempered."

Joseph Hunter was a carpenter, Robert Burns a ploughman, Keats a druggist, Thomas Carlyle a mason, Hugh Miller a stone mason. Rubens, the artist, was a page, Swedenborg, a mining engineer. Dante and Descartes were soldiers. Ben Johnson was a brick layer and worked at building Lincoln Inn in London with trowel in hand and a book in his pocket. Jeremy Taylor was a barber. Andrew Johnson was a tailor. Cardinal Wolsey was a butcher's son. So were Defoe and Kirke White. Michael Faraday was the son of a blacksmith. He even excelled his teacher, Sir Humphry Davy, who was an apprentice to an apothecary.

Virgil was the son of a porter, Homer of a farmer, Pope of a merchant, Horace of a shopkeeper, Demosthenes of a cutler, Milton of a money scrivener, Shakespeare of a wool stapler, and Oliver Cromwell of a brewer.

John Wanamaker's first salary was $1.25 per week. A. T. Stewart began his business life as a school teacher. James Keene drove a milk wagon in a California town. Joseph Pulitzer, proprietor of the New York *World*, once acted as stoker on a Mississippi steamboat. When a young man, Cyrus Field was a clerk in a New England store. George W. Childs was an errand boy for a bookseller at $4 a month. Andrew Carnegie began work in a Pittsburg telegraph office at $3 a week. C. P. Huntington sold butter and eggs for what he could get a pound or dozen. Whitelaw Reid was once a correspondent of a newspaper in Cincinnati at $5 per week. Adam Forepaugh was once a butcher in Philadelphia.

Sarah Bernhardt was a dressmaker's apprentice. Adelaide Neilson began life as a child's nurse. Miss Braddon, the novelist, was a utility actress in the provinces. Charlotte Cushman was the daughter of poor people.

Mr. W. O. Stoddard, in his "Men of Business," tells a characteristic story of the late Leland Stanford. When eighteen years of age his father purchased a tract of woodland, but had not the means to clear it as he wished. He told

Leland that he could have all he could make from the timber if he would leave the land clear of trees. A new market had just then been created for cord wood, and Leland took some money that he had saved, hired other choppers to help him, and sold over two thousand cords of wood to the Mohawk and Hudson River Railroad at a net profit of $2600. He used this sum to start him in his law studies, and thus, as Mr. Stoddard says, chopped his way to the bar.

It is said that the career of Benjamin Franklin is full of inspiration for any young man. When he left school for good he was only twelve years of age. At first he did little but read. He soon found, however, that reading, alone, would not make him an educated man, and he proceeded to act upon this discovery at once. At school he had been unable to understand arithmetic. Twice he had given it up as a hopeless puzzle, and finally left school almost hopelessly ignorant upon the subject. But the printer's boy soon found his ignorance of figures extremely inconvenient. When he was about fourteen he took up for the *third time* the "Cocker's Arithmetic," *which had baffled him at school,* and*ciphered all through it with ease and pleasure.* He then mastered a work upon navigation, which included the rudiments of geometry, and thus tasted "the inexhaustible charm of mathematics." He pursued a similar course, we are told, in acquiring the art of composition, in which, at length, he excelled most of the men of his time. When he was but a boy of sixteen, he wrote so well that the pieces which he slyly sent to his brother's paper were thought to have been written by some of the most learned men in the colony.

Henry Clay, the "mill-boy of the slashes," was one of seven children of a widow too poor to send him to any but a common country school, where he was drilled only in the "three R's." But he used every spare moment to study without a teacher, and in after years he was a king among self-made men.

The most successful man is he who has triumphed over obstacles, disadvantages and discouragements.

It is Goodyear in his rude laboratory enduring poverty and failure until the pasty rubber is at length hardened; it is Edison biding his time in baggage car and in printing office until that mysterious light and power glows and throbs at his command; it is Carey on his cobbler's bench nourishing the great purpose that at length carried the message of love to benighted India;—these are the cases and examples of true success.

CHAPTER IV

OUT OF PLACE

The high prize of life, the crowning fortune of a man, is to be born with a bias to some pursuit, which finds him in employment and happiness.—EMERSON.

The art of putting the right man in the right place is perhaps the first in the science of government, but the art of finding a satisfactory position for the discontented is the most difficult.—TALLEYRAND.

It is a celebrated thought of Socrates, that if all the misfortunes of mankind were cast into a public stock, in order to be equally distributed among the whole species, those who now think themselves the most unhappy would prefer the share they are already possessed of, before that which would fall to them by such a division.—ADDISON.

I was born to other things.—TENNYSON.

How many a rustic Milton has passed by,Stifling the speechless longings of his heart,In unremitting drudgery and care!How many a vulgar Cato has compelledHis energies, no longer tameless then,To mould a pin, or fabricate a nail.—SHELLEY.

"But I'm good for something," pleaded a young man whom a merchant was about to discharge for his bluntness. "You are good for nothing as a salesman," said his employer. "I am sure I can be useful," said the youth. "How? Tell me how." "I don't know, sir, I don't know." "Nor do I," said the merchant, laughing at the earnestness of his clerk. "Only don't put me away, sir, don't put me away. Try me at something besides selling. I cannot sell; I know I cannot sell." "I know that, too," said the principal; "that is what is wrong." "But I can make myself useful somehow," persisted the young man; "I know I can." He was placed in the counting-house, where his aptitude for figures soon showed itself, and in a few years he became not only chief cashier in the large store, but an eminent accountant.

"Out of an art," says Bulwer, "a man may be so trivial you would mistake him for an imbecile—at best, a grown infant. Put him into his art, and how high he soars above you! How quietly he enters into a heaven of which he has become a denizen, and unlocking the gates with his golden key, admits you to follow, an humble reverent visitor."

A man out of place is like a fish out of water. Its fins mean nothing, they are only a hindrance. The fish can do nothing but flounder out of its element. But as soon as the fins feel the water, they mean something. Fifty-two per cent of our college graduates studied law, not because, in many cases, they have the slightest natural aptitude for it, but because it is put down as the proper road to promotion.

A man never grows in personal power and moral stamina when out of his place. If he grows at all, it is a narrow, one-sided, stunted growth, not a manly growth. Nature abhors the slightest perversion of natural aptitude or deviation from the sealed orders which accompany every soul into this world.

A man out of place is not half a man. He feels unmanned, unsexed. He cannot respect himself, hence he cannot be respected.

You can enter all kinds of horses for a race, but only those which have natural adaptation for speed will make records; the others will only make themselves ridiculous by their lumbering, unnatural exertions to win. How many truck and family-horse lawyers make themselves ridiculous by trying to speed on the law track, where courts and juries only laugh at them. The effort to redeem themselves from scorn may enable them by unnatural exertions to become fairly passable, but the same efforts along the line of their strength or adaptation would make them kings in their line.

"Jonathan," said Mr. Chace, when his son told of having nearly fitted himself for college, "thou shalt go down to the machine-shop on Monday morning." It was many years before Jonathan escaped from the shop to work his way up to the position of a man of great influence as a United States Senator from Rhode Island.

Galileo was sent to the university at Pisa at seventeen, with the strict injunction not to neglect medical subjects for the alluring study of philosophy or literature. But when he was eighteen he discovered the great principle of the pendulum by a lamp left swinging in the cathedral.

John Adams' father was a shoemaker; and, trying to teach his son the art, gave him some "uppers" to cut out by a pattern which had a three-cornered hole in it to hang it up by. The future statesman followed the pattern, hole and all.

There is a tradition that Tennyson's first poems were published at the instigation of his father's coachman. His grandfather gave the lad ten shillings for writing an elegy on his grandmother. As he handed it to him, he said; "There, that's the first money you ever earned by your poetry, and take my word for it, it will be the last."

Murillo's mother had marked her boy for a priest, but nature had already laid her hand upon him and marked him for her own. His mother was shocked on returning from church one day to find that the child had taken down the sacred family picture, "Jesus and the Lamb," and had painted his own hat on the Saviour's head, and had changed the lamb into a dog.

The poor boy's home was broken up, and he started out on foot and alone to seek his fortune. All he had was courage and determination to make something of himself. He not only became a famous artist, but a man of great character.

"Let us people who are so uncommonly clever and learned," says Thackeray, "have a great tenderness and pity for the folks who are not endowed with the prodigious talents which we have. I have always had a regard for dunces,— those of my own school days were among the pleasantest of the fellows, and have turned out by no means the dullest in life; whereas, many a youth who could turn off Latin hexameters by the yard, and construe Greek quite glibly, is no better than a feeble prig now, with not a pennyworth more brains than were in his head before his beard grew."

"In the winter of 1824, there set in a great flood upon the town of Sidmouth, the tide rose to a terrible height. In the midst of this sublime and terrible storm, Dame Partington, who lived upon the beach, was seen at the door of her house, with mop and pattens, trundling her mop, squeezing out the sea-water, and vigorously pushing away the Atlantic Ocean. The Atlantic was roused. Mrs. Partington's spirit was up: but I need not tell you the contest was unequal; the Atlantic Ocean beat Mrs. Partington. She was excellent at a slop or a puddle, but she should not have meddled with a tempest."

How many Dame Partingtons there are of both sexes, and in every walk of life!

The young swan is restless and uneasy until she finds the element she has never before seen. Then,

"With archéd neckBetween her white wings mantling proudly, rowsHer state with oary feet."

What a wretched failure was that of Haydon the painter. He thought he failed through the world's ingratitude or injustice, but his failure was due wholly to his being out of place. His bitter disappointments at his half successes were really pitiable because to him they were more than failures. He had not the slightest sense of color, yet went through life under the delusion that he was an artist.

"If it is God's will to take any of my children by death, I hope it may be Isaac," said the father of Dr. Isaac Barrow. "Why do you tell that blockhead the same thing twenty times over?" asked John Wesley's father. "Because," replied his mother, "if I had told him but nineteen times, all my labor would have been lost, while now he will understand and remember."

A man out of place may manage to get a living, but he has lost the buoyancy, energy and enthusiasm which are as natural to a man in his place as his breath. He is industrious, but he works mechanically and without heart. It is to support himself and family, *not because he cannot help it.* Dinner time does not come two hours before he realizes it; a man out of place is constantly looking at his watch and thinking of his salary.

If a man is in his place he is happy, joyous, cheerful, energetic, fertile in resources. The days are all too short for him. All his faculties give their consent to his work; say "yes" to his occupation. He is a man; he respects himself and is happy because all his powers are at play in their natural sphere. There is no compromising of his faculties, no cramping of legal acumen upon the farm; no suppressing of forensic oratorical powers at the shoemaker's bench; no stifling of exuberance of physical strength, of visions of golden crops and blooded cattle amid the loved country life in the dry clergyman's study, composing sermons to put the congregation to sleep.

To be out of place is demoralizing to all the powers of manhood. We can't cheat nature out of her aim; if she has set all the currents of your life toward medicine or law, you will only be a botch at anything else. Will-power and application cannot make a farmer of a born painter any more than a lumbering draught horse can be changed into a race horse. When the powers are not used along the line of their strength they become demoralized, weakened, deteriorated. Self-respect, enthusiasm and courage ooze out; we become half-hearted and success is impossible.

Scott was called the great blockhead while in Edinburgh College. Grant's mother called the future General and President, "Useless Grant," because he was so unhandy and dull.

Erskine had at length found his place as a lawyer; he carried everything before him at the bar. Had he remained in the navy he would probably never have been heard from. When elected to Parliament, his lofty spirit was chilled by the cold sarcasm and contemptuous indifference of Pitt, whom he was expected by his friends to annihilate. But he was again out of his place; he was shorn of his magic power and his eloquent tongue faltered from a consciousness of being out of his place.

Gould failed as a storekeeper, tanner and surveyor and civil engineer, before he got into a railroad office where he "struck his gait."

When extracts from James Russell Lowell's poem at Harvard were shown his father at Rome, instead of being pleased the latter said, "James promised me when I left home, that he would give up poetry and stick to books. I had hoped that he had become less flighty." The world is full of people at war with their positions.

Man only grows when he is developing along the lines of his own individuality, and not when he is trying to be somebody else. All attempts to imitate another man, when there is no one like you in all creation, as the pattern was broken when you were born, is not only to ruin your own pattern, but to make only an echo of the one imitated. There is no strength off the lines of our own individuality.

Anywhere else we are dwarfs, weaklings, echoes, and the echo even of a great man is a sorry contrast to even the smallest human being who is himself.

CHAPTER V

WHAT SHALL I DO?

No man ever made an ill-figure who understood his own talents, nor a good one who mistook them.—SWIFT.

Blessed is he who has found his work,—let him ask no other blessing.—CARLYLE.

Whatever you are by nature, keep to it; never desert your line of talent. Be what nature intended you for, and you will succeed; be anything else, and you will be ten thousand times worse than nothing.—SYDNEY SMITH.

He who is false to present duty breaks a thread in the loom, and will find the flaw when he may have forgotten its cause.—BEECHER.

I am glad to thinkI am not bound to make the world go round;But only to discover and to do,With cheerful heart, the work that God appoints.—JEAN INGELOW.

"Do that which is assigned you," says Emerson, "and you cannot hope too much or dare too much. There is at this moment for you an utterance brave and grand as that of the colossal chisel of Phidias, or trowel of the Egyptians, or the pen of Moses or Dante, but different from all these."

"I felt that I was in the world to do something, and thought I must," said Whittier, thus giving the secret of his great power. It is the man who must enter law, literature, medicine, the ministry, or any other of the overstocked professions, who will succeed. His certain call—that is, his love for it, and his fidelity to it—are the imperious factors of his career. If a man enters a profession simply because his grandfather made a great name in it, or his mother wants him to, with no love or adaptability for it, it were far better for him to be a day laborer. In the humbler work, his intelligence may make him a leader; in the other career he might do as much harm as a boulder rolled from its place upon a railroad track, a menace to the next express.

Lowell said: "It is the vain endeavor to make ourselves what we are not, that has strewn history with so many broken purposes, and lives left in the rough."

"The age has no aversion to preaching as such," said Phillips Brooks, "it may not listen to your preaching." But though it may not listen to your preaching, it will wear your boots, or buy your flour, or see stars through your telescope. It has a use for every person, and it is his business to find out what that use is.

The following advertisement appeared several times in a paper without bringing a letter:

"WANTED.—Situation by a Practical Printer, who is competent to take charge of any department in a printing and publishing house. Would accept a professorship in any of the academies. Has no objection to teach ornamental painting and penmanship, geometry, trigonometry, and many other sciences. Has had some experience as a lay preacher. Would have no objection to form a small class of young ladies and gentlemen to instruct them in the higher branches. To a dentist or chiropodist he would be invaluable; or he would cheerfully accept a position as bass or tenor singer in a choir."

At length there appeared this addition to the notice:

"P.S. Will accept an offer to saw and split wood at less than the usual rates."

This secured a situation at once, and the advertisement was seen no more.

Don't wait for a higher position or a larger salary. Enlarge the position you already occupy; put originality of method into it. Fill it as it never was filled before. Be more prompt, more energetic, more thorough, more polite than your predecessor or fellow-workmen. Study your business, devise new modes of operation, be able to give your employer points. The art lies not in giving satisfaction merely, not in simply filling your place, but in doing better than was expected, in surprising your employer; and the reward will be a better place and a larger salary.

"He that hath a trade," says Franklin, "hath an estate; and he that hath a calling hath a place of profit and honor. A ploughman on his legs is higher than a gentleman on his knees."

Follow your bent. You cannot long fight successfully against your aspirations. Parents, friends, or misfortune may stifle and suppress the longings of the heart, by compelling you to perform unwelcome tasks; but, like a volcano, the inner fire will burst the crusts which confine it and pour forth its pent-up genius in eloquence, in song, in art, or in some favorite industry. Beware of "a talent which you cannot hope to practice in perfection." Nature hates all botched and half-finished work, and will pronounce her curse upon it.

Your talent is your *call*. Your legitimate destiny speaks in your character.

If you have found your place, your occupation has the consent of every faculty of your being.

If possible, choose that occupation which focuses the largest amount of your experience and tastes. You will then not only have a congenial vocation, but will utilize largely your skill and business knowledge, which is your true capital.

There is no doubt that every person has a special adaptation for his own peculiar part in life. A very few—the geniuses, we call them—have this marked in an unusual degree, and very early in life.

A man's business does more to make him than anything else. It hardens his muscles, strengthens his body, quickens his blood, sharpens his mind, corrects his judgment, wakes up his inventive genius, puts his wits to work, starts him on the race of life, arouses his ambition, makes him feel that he is a man and must fill a man's shoes, do a man's work, bear a man's part in life, and show himself a man in that part. No man feels himself a man who is not doing a man's business. A man without employment is not a man. He does not prove by his works that he is a man. A hundred and fifty pounds of bone and muscle do not make a man. A good cranium full of brains is not a man. The bone and muscle and brain must know how to do a man's work, think a man's thoughts, mark out a man's path, and bear a man's weight of character and duty before they constitute a man.

Whatever you do in life, be greater than your calling. Most people look upon an occupation or calling as a mere expedient for earning a living. What a mean, narrow view to take of what was intended for the great school of life, the great man-developer, the character-builder; that which should broaden, deepen, heighten, and round out into symmetry, harmony and beauty, all the God-given faculties within us! How we shrink from the task and evade the lessons which were intended for the unfolding of life's great possibilities into usefulness and power, as the sun unfolds into beauty and fragrance the petals of the flower.

"Girls, you cheapen yourselves by lack of purpose in life," says Rena L. Miner. "You show commendable zeal in pursuing your studies; your alertness in comprehending and ability in surmounting difficult problems have become proverbial; nine times out of ten you outrank your brothers thus far; but when the end is attained, the goal reached, whether it be the graduating certificate from a graded school, or a college diploma, for nine out of every ten it might as well be added thereto, 'dead to further activity,' or, 'sleeping until marriage shall resurrect her.'

"Crocheting, placquing, dressing, visiting, music, and flirtations, make up the sum total for the expense and labor expended for your existence. If forced to earn your support, you are content to stand behind a counter, or teach school term after term in the same grade, while the young men who graduated with you walk up the grades, as up a ladder, to professorship and good salary, from which they swing off into law, physics, or perhaps the legislative firmament, leaving difficulties and obstacles like nebulæ in their wake.—You girls, satisfied with mediocrity, have an eye mainly for the 'main chance'—marriage. If you marry wealthy,—which is marrying well according to the modern popular idea,—you dress more elegantly, cultivate more fashionable society, leave your thinking for your husband and your minister to do for you, and become in the economy of life but a sentient nonentity. If you are true to the grand passion, and accept with it poverty, you bake, brew, scrub, spank the children, and talk with your neighbor over the back fence for recreation, spending the years literally like the horse in a treadmill, all for the lack of a purpose,—a purpose sufficiently potent to convert the latent talent into a gem of living beauty, a creative force which makes all adjuncts secondary, like planets to their central sun. Choose some one course or calling, and master it in all its details, sleep by it, swear by it, work for it, and, if marriage crowns you, it can but add new glory to your labor."

Dr. Hall says that the world has urgent need of "girls who are mother's right hand; girls who can cuddle the little ones next best to mamma, and smooth out the tangles in the domestic skein when things get twisted; girls whom father takes comfort in for something better than beauty, and the big brothers are proud of for something that outranks the ability to dance or shine in society. Next, we want girls of sense,—girls who have a standard of their own regardless of conventionalities, and are independent enough to live up to it; girls who simply won't wear a trailing dress on the street to gather up microbes and all sorts of defilement; girls who don't wear a high hat to the theatre, or lacerate their feet with high heels and endanger their health with corsets; girls who will wear what is pretty and becoming and snap their fingers at the dictates of fashion when fashion is horrid and silly. And we want good girls,—girls who are sweet, right straight out from the heart to the lips; innocent and pure and simple girls, with less knowledge of sin and duplicity and evil-doing at twenty than the pert little schoolgirl of ten has all too often. And we want careful girls and prudent girls, who think enough of the generous father who toils to maintain them in comfort, and of the gentle mother who denies herself much that they may have so many pretty things, to count the cost and draw the line between the essentials and non-essentials; girls who strive to save and not to spend; girls who are unselfish and eager to be a joy and a comfort in the home rather than an expense and a useless burden. We want girls with hearts,—girls who are full of tenderness and sympathy, with tears that flow for other people's ills, and smiles that light outward their own beautiful thoughts. We have lots of clever girls, and brilliant girls, and witty girls. Give us a consignment of jolly girls, warm-hearted and impulsive girls; kind and entertaining to their own folks, and with little desire to shine in the garish world. With a few such girls scattered around, life would freshen up for all of us, as the weather does under the spell of summer showers."

CHAPTER VI

WILL YOU PAY THE PRICE?

The gods sell anything and to everybody at a fair price.—EMERSON.

All desire knowledge, but no one is willing to pay the price.—JUVENAL.

There is no royal path which leads to geometry.—EUCLID.

There is no road to success but through a clear, strong purpose. A purpose underlies character, culture, position, attainment of whatever sort.—T. T. MUNGER.

Remember you have not a sinew whose law of strength is not action; you have not a faculty of body, mind, or soul, whose law of improvement is not energy.—E. B. HALL.

"We have but what we make, and every goodIs locked by nature in a granite hand,Sheer labor must unclench."

"Oh, if I could thus put a dream on canvas!" exclaimed an enthusiastic young artist, pointing to a most beautiful painting. "Dream on canvas!" growled the master, "it is the ten thousand touches with the brush you must learn to put on canvas that make your dream."

"There is but one method of attaining excellence," said Sydney Smith, "and that is hard labor."

"If only Milton's imagination could have conceived his visions," says Waters, "his consummate industry alone could have carved the immortal lines which enshrine them. If only Newton's mind could reach out to the secrets of nature, even his genius could only do it by the homeliest toil. The works of Bacon are not midsummer-night's dreams, but, like coral islands, they have risen from the depths of truth, and formed their broad surfaces above the ocean by the minutest accretions of persevering labor. The conceptions of Michael Angelo would have perished like a night's phantasy, had not his industry given them permanence."

Salvini contributes the following to the *Century* as to his habits of study before he had established himself as a past master of tragedy: "I imposed upon myself a new method of study. While I was busying myself with the part of Saul, I read and reread the Bible, so as to become impregnated with the appropriate sentiments, manners and local color. When I took up Othello, I pored over the history of the Venetian Republic and that of the Moorish invasion of Spain. I studied the passions of the Moors, their art of war, their religious beliefs, nor did I overlook the romance of Giraldi Cinthio, in order the better to master that sublime character. I did not concern myself about a superficial study of the words, or of some point of scenic effect, or of greater or less accentuation of certain phrases with a view to win passing applause; a vaster horizon opened out before me—an infinite sea on which my bark could navigate in security, without fear of falling in with reefs."

His method was not new, but he considered it so, and gives his opinion in quotation-marks. He speaks of characters with which, his name is not always associated by writers on the stage, but is correct, I think, in the main.

Many years ago a little boy entered Harrow school and was put in a class beyond his years, wherein all the other boys had the advantage of previous instruction. His master used to reprove his dullness, but all his efforts could not raise him from the lowest place in the class. The boy finally procured the elementary books which the other boys had studied. He devoted the hours of play and many of the hours of sleep to mastering the elementary principles of these books. This boy was soon at the head of his class and the pride of Harrow. The statue of that boy, Sir William Jones, stands to-day in St. Paul's Cathedral; for he lived to be the greatest Oriental scholar of Europe.

"What is the secret of success in business?" asked a friend of Cornelius Vanderbilt. "Secret! there is no secret about it," replied the commodore; "all you have to do is to attend to your business and go ahead." If you would adopt Vanderbilt's method, know your business, attend to it, and keep down expenses until your fortune is safe from business perils.

"Work or starve," is nature's motto,—and it is written on the stars and the sod alike,—starve mentally, starve morally, starve physically. It is an inexorable law of nature that whatever is not used, dies. "Nothing for nothing," is her maxim. If we are idle and shiftless by choice, we shall be nerveless and powerless by necessity.

The mottoes of great men often give us glimpses of the secret of their characters and success. "Work! work! work!" was the motto of Sir Joshua Reynolds, David Wilkie, and scores of other men who have left their mark upon the world. Voltaire's motto was "Toujours au travail" (always at work). Scott's maxim was "Never be doing nothing." Michael Angelo was a wonderful worker. He even slept in his clothes ready to spring to his work as soon as he awoke. He kept a block of marble in his bedroom that he might get up in the night and work when he could not sleep. His favorite device was an old man in a go-cart, with an hour-glass upon it, bearing this inscription: "Ancora imparo" (still I'm learning). Even after he was blind he would ask to be wheeled into the Belvidere, to examine the statues with his hands. Cobden used to say, "I'm working like a horse without a moment to spare." It was said that Handel, the musician, did the work of a dozen men. Nothing ever daunted him. He feared neither ridicule nor defeat. Lord Palmerston worked like a slave, even in his old age. Being asked when he considered a man in his prime, he replied, "Seventy-nine," that being his own age. Humboldt was one of the world's great workers. In summer he arose at four in the morning for thirty years. He used to say work was as much of a necessity as eating or sleeping. Sir Walter Scott was a phenomenal worker. He wrote the "Waverley Novels" at the rate of twelve volumes a year. He averaged a volume every two months during his whole working life. What an example is this to the young men of to-day, of the possibilities of an earnest life! Edmund Burke was one of the most prodigious workers that ever lived.

George Stephenson used to work at meal time, getting out loads of coal while the miners were at dinner in order that he might earn a few extra shillings to buy a spelling-book and an arithmetic. His associates thought he was very foolish, and asked him what good it would do to learn to read and cipher. He told them he was determined to improve his mind; so he studied whenever he could snatch a minute before the engine's fire, and in every possible situation until he had a good, practical, common-sense education.

Garibaldi's father decided that Guiseppe should be a minister, because the boy was so sorry for a cricket which lost its leg. Samuel Morse's father concluded that his son would preach well because he could not keep his head above water in a dangerous attempt to catch bait in the Mystic River. President Dwight told young Morse he would never make a painter, and hinted that he never would amount to much any way if he did not study more. Although under the teaching of West and Allston in London, he became a tolerable portrait painter, he did not find his sphere until returning from England on a sailing vessel, he heard Professor Jackson explain an electrical experiment in Paris, when the thought of the telegraph flashed into his mind and he found no rest, until he flashed over the wire the first message, "What hath God wrought!" on the experimental line between Baltimore and Washington: this was May 24, 1844.

William H. Vanderbilt was by far the wealthiest man in the world. Chauncey M. Depew estimated his fortune at two hundred millions. He left his eight children ten millions each, except Cornelius and William K., who had sixty-five millions each. Commodore Vanderbilt, his father, amassed a fortune of eighty millions of dollars in his own lifetime, and that too at a time when it was more difficult to make money than it is now.

Mr. C. P. Huntington is a good example of a self-made man. His father was a Connecticut farmer. The farm was left to him, but he traded it off for a lot of clocks which he peddled in mining districts for gold dust and nuggets. He and Mark Hopkins formed a partnership and opened a hardware store in California. They united with Leland Stanford in the construction of a railroad, and they all got rich rapidly. Mr. Huntington is one of the greatest railroad operators of the country. He always acted upon the principle that he would control the stock of any road in which he was interested. He is one of the most methodical men of all the millionaires of this country. He is very plain in his manner, strictly temperate, and very abstemious in his living. He said he never knew what it was to be tired.

Russell Sage used to keep a grocery store in Troy, N. Y. He finally associated himself with Jay Gould, who used to be a constant borrower of money of him. Mr. Sage probably keeps more ready money on hand than any other millionaire. He can nearly always control ten millions or more at call. He has never speculated in stocks to any extent. Mr. Sage's word is as good as any bond. He has no taste for ordinary diversions, except driving.

Philip D. Armour, who has the appearance of a prosperous farmer, was born on a farm near Watertown, N. J. He became fired with a desire to see the "Boundless West." His mind seemed to run to hogs, and with a financial instinct he made up his mind that there was a fortune in transporting the hogs from where they were so plenty to where there were so few of them and so many to eat them. He could now purchase every hog in the world and then have money left to buy a railroad or two.

Mrs. Hetty Green is probably the richest woman in the world. Her fortune has grown from the little industry of her father in New Bedford, Mass. She has raised the nine millions left her by her father and nine millions left her by her aunt to thirty millions. She is a woman of great ability and courage. She once took with her five millions of dollars of securities in a satchel on a street car to deposit with her banker on Wall street.

The probabilities are that billionaires will be as plentiful in the twentieth century as millionaires are to-day, through hard work, self-denial, rigid economy, method, accuracy, and strict temperance, for not one of the self-made millionaires are intemperate. John D. Rockefeller never tastes intoxicating liquor. He seems as unvarying in his method and system as the laws of the universe. Jay Gould did not use wine or intoxicating liquor of any kind. Mr. Huntington does not even drink coffee, while William Waldorf Astor merely takes a sip of wine for courtesy's sake. Not one of the leading millionaires uses tobacco, and not one of them is profane. Very rich men are almost always honest in their dealings, so far as their word is concerned. William Waldorf Astor, until recently, has been considered the richest man in the world, but John D. Rockefeller surpasses him now, it is said. The whole wealth of Crœsus was little more than the income of this modern Crœsus for one year. Mr. Rockefeller controls about eighty or ninety millions of capital stock in the Standard Oil Trust. The Standard Oil Company is one of the best managed corporations in the world.

Two centuries and a quarter ago, a little, tempest-tossed, weather-beaten bark, barely escaped from the jaws of the wild Atlantic, landed upon the bleakest shore of New England. From her deck disembarked a hundred and one careworn exiles.

To the casual observer no event could seem more insignificant. The contemptuous eye of the world scarcely deigned to notice it. Yet the famous vessel that bore Cæsar and his fortunes, carried but an ignoble freight compared with that of the Mayflower. Though landed by a treacherous pilot upon a barren and inhospitable coast, they sought neither richer fields nor a more congenial climate, but liberty and opportunity.

A lady once asked Turner the secret of his great success.

"I have no secret, madam, but hard work."

"This is a secret that many never learn, and they don't succeed because they fail to learn it. Labor is the genius that changes the world from ugliness to beauty, and the great curse to a great blessing."

See Balzac, in his lonely garret, toiling, toiling, waiting, waiting, amid poverty and hunger, but neither hunger, debt, poverty nor discouragement could induce him to swerve a hair's breadth from his purpose. He could wait, even while a world scoffed.

"Mankind is more indebted to industry than to ingenuity," says Addison; "the gods set up their favors at a price and industry is the purchaser."

Rome was a mighty nation while industry led her people, but when her great conquests of wealth and slaves placed her citizens above work, that moment her glory began to fade, and vice and corruption, induced by idleness, doomed the proud city to an ignominious history. Even Cicero, Rome's great orator, said, "All artisans are engaged in a disgraceful occupation;" and Aristotle said, "The best regulated states will not permit a mechanic to be a citizen, for it is impossible for one who lives the life of a mechanic, or hired servant, to practice a life of virtue. Some were born to be slaves." But, fortunately there came a mightier than Rome, Cicero or Aristotle, whose magnificent life and example forever lifted the false ban from labor and redeemed it from disgrace. He gave dignity to the most menial service, and significance to labor.

Christ did not say, "Come unto me all ye pleasure hunters, ye indolent and ye lazy;" but "Come all ye that *labor* and are *heavy laden.*"

Columbus was a persistent and practical, as well as an intellectual hero. He went from one state to another, urging kings and emperors to undertake the first visiting of a world which his instructed spirit already discerned in the far-off seas. He first tried his own countrymen at Genoa, but found none ready to help him. He then went to Portugal, and submitted his project to John II., who laid it before his council. It was scouted as extravagant and chimerical.

Nevertheless, the king endeavored to steal Columbus's idea. A fleet was sent forth in the direction indicated by the navigator, but, being frustrated by storms and winds, it returned to Lisbon after four days' voyaging.

Columbus returned to Genoa, and again renewed his propositions to the Republic, but without success. Nothing discouraged him. The finding of the New World was the irrevocable object of his life. He went to Spain, and landed at the town of Palos, in Andalusia. He went by chance to a convent of Franciscans, knocked at the door and asked for a little bread and water. The prior gratefully received the stranger, enter tained him, and learned from him the story of his life. He encouraged him in his hopes, and furnished him with an admission to the Court of Spain, then at Cordova. King Ferdinand received him graciously, but before coming to a decision he desired to lay the project before a council of his wisest men at Salamanca. Columbus had to reply, not only to the scientific arguments laid before him, but to citations from the Bible. The Spanish clergy declared that the theory of the antipodes was hostile to the faith. The earth, they said, was an immense flat disk; and if there was a new earth beyond the ocean, then all men could not be descended from Adam. *Columbus was considered a fool.*

Still bent on his idea, he wrote to the King of England, then to the King of France, without effect. At last, in 1492, Columbus was introduced by Louis de Saint Angel to Queen Isabella of Spain. The friends who accompanied him pleaded his cause with so much force and conviction that he at length persuaded the queen to aid him.

Lord Ellenborough was a great worker. He had a very hard time in getting a start at the bar, but was determined never to relax his industry until success came to him. When he was worked down to absolute exhaustion, he had this card which he kept constantly before his eyes, lest he might be tempted to relax his efforts: "Read or Starve."

Show me a man who has made fifty thousand dollars, and I will show you in that man an equivalent of energy, attention to detail, trustworthiness, punctuality, professional knowledge, good address, common sense, and other marketable qualities. The farmer respects his savings bank book not unnaturally, for it declares with all the solemnity of a sealed and stamped document that for a certain length of time he rose at six o'clock each morning to oversee his labors, that he patiently waited upon seasonable weather, that he understood buying and selling. To the medical man, his fee serves as a medal to indicate that he was brave enough to face small pox and other infectious diseases, and his self-respect is fostered thereby.

The barrister's brief is marked with the price of his legal knowledge, of his eloquence, or of his brave endurance during a period of hope-deferred brieflessness.

A rich man asked Howard Burnett to do a little thing for his album. Burnett complied and charged a thousand francs. "But it took you only five minutes," objected the rich man. "Yes, but it took me thirty years to learn how to do it in five minutes."

"I prepared that sermon," said a young sprig of divinity, "in half an hour, and preached it at once, and thought nothing of it." "In that," said an older minister, "your hearers are at one with you, for they also thought nothing of it."

Virgil seems to have accomplished about four lines a week; but then they have lasted eighteen hundred years and will last eighteen hundred more.

Seven years Virgil is said to have expended in the composition of the Georgics, and they could all be printed in about seven columns of an ordinary newspaper. Tradition reports that he was in the habit of composing a few lines in the morning and spending the rest of the day in polishing them. Campbell used to say that if a poet made one good line a week, he did very well indeed; but Moore thought that if a poet did his duty, he could get a line done every day.

What an army of young men enters the success-contest every year as raw recruits! Many of them are country youths flocking to the cities to buy success. Their young ambitions have been excited by some book, or fired by the story of some signal success, and they dream of becoming Astors or Girards, Stewarts or Wanamakers, Vanderbilts or Goulds, Lincolns or Garfields, until their innate energy impels them to try their own fortune in the magic metropolis. But what are you willing to pay for "success," as you call it, young man? Do you realize what that word means in a great city in the nineteenth century, where men grow gray at thirty and die of old age at forty,—where the race of life has become so intense that the runners are treading on the heels of those before them; and "woe to him who stops to tie his shoestring?" Do you know that only two or three out of every hundred will ever win permanent success, and only because they have kept everlastingly at it; and that the rest will sooner or later fail and many die in poverty because they have given up the struggle.

There are multitudes of men who never rely wholly upon themselves and achieve independence. They are like summer vines, which never grow even ligneous, but stretch out a thousand little hands to grasp the stronger shrubs; and if they cannot reach them, they lie dishevelled in the grass, hoof-trodden, and beaten of every storm. It will be found that the first real movement upward will not take place until, in a spirit of resolute self-denial, indolence, so natural to almost every one, is mastered. Necessity is, usually, the spur that sets the sluggish energies in motion. Poverty, therefore, is often of inestimable value as an incentive to the best endeavors of which we are capable.

CHAPTER VII

FOUNDATION STONES

In all matters, before beginning, a diligent preparation should be made.—CICERO.

How great soever a genius may be, ... certain it is that he will never shine in his full lustre, nor shed the full influence he is capable of, unless to his own experience he adds that of other men and other ages.—BOLINGBROKE.

It is for want of the little that human means must add to the wonderful capacity for improvement, born in man, that by far the greatest part of the intellect, innate in our race, perishes undeveloped and unknown.—EDWARD EVERETT.

If any man fancies that there is some easier way of gaining a dollar than by squarely earning it, he has lost his clue to his way through this mortal labyrinth and must henceforth wander as chance may dictate.—HORACE GREELEY.

What we do upon some great occasion will probably depend on what we already are; and what we are will be the result of previous years of self-discipline.—H. P. LIDDON.

Learn to labor and to wait.—LONGFELLOW.

"What avails all this sturdiness?" asked an oak tree which had grown solitary for two hundred years, bitterly handled by frosts and wrestled by winds. "Why am I to stand here useless? My roots are anchored in rifts of rocks; no herds can lie down under my shadow; I am far above singing birds, that seldom come to rest among my leaves; I am set as a mark for storms, that bend and tear me; my fruit is serviceable for no appetite; it had been better for me to have been a mushroom, gathered in the morning for some poor man's table, than to be a hundred-year oak, good for nothing."

While it yet spoke, the axe was hewing at its base. It died in sadness, saying as it fell, "Weary ages for nothing have I lived."

The axe completed its work. By and by the trunk and root form the knees of a stately ship, bearing the country's flag around the world. Other parts form keel and ribs of merchantmen, and having defied the mountain storms, they now equally resist the thunder of the waves and the murky threat of scowling hurricanes. Other parts are laid into floors, or wrought into wainscoting, or carved for frames of noble pictures, or fashioned into chairs that embosom the weakness of old age. Thus the tree, in dying, came not to its end, but to its beginning of life. It voyaged the world. It grew to parts of temples and dwellings.

It held upon its surface the soft tread of children and the tottering steps of patriarchs. It rocked in the cradle. It swayed the limbs of age by the chimney corner, and heard, secure within, the roar of those old, unwearied tempests that once surged about its mountain life. All its early struggles and hardships had enabled it to grow tough and hard and beautiful of grain, alike useful and ornamental.

"Sir, you have been to college, I presume?" asked an illiterate but boastful exhorter of a clergyman. "Yes, sir," was the reply. "I am thankful," said the former, "that the Lord opened my mouth without any learning." "A similar event," retorted the clergyman, "happened in Balaam's time."

Why not allow the schoolboy to erase from his list of studies all subjects that appear to him useless? Would he not erase every thing which taxed his pleasure and freedom? Would he not obey the call of his blood, rather than the advice of his teacher? Ignorant men who have made money tell him that the study of geography is useless; his tea will come over the sea to him whether he knows where China is or not; what difference does it make whether verbs agree with their subjects or not? Why waste time learning geometry or algebra? Who keeps accounts by these? Learning spoils a man for business, they tell him; they begrudge the time and money spent in education. They want cheap and rapid transit through college for their children. Veneer will answer every practical purpose for them, instead of solid mahogany, or even paint and pine will do.

It is said that the editors of the Dictionary of American Biography who diligently searched the records of living and dead Americans, found 15,142 names worthy of a place in their six volumes of annals of successful men, and 5326, or more than one-third of them, were college-educated men. One in forty of the college educated attained a success worthy of mention, and but one in 10,000 of those not so educated; so that the college-bred man had two hundred and fifty times the chances for success that others had. Medical records, it is said, show that but five per cent. of the practicing physicians of the United States are college graduates; and yet forty-six per cent. of the physicians who became locally famous enough to be mentioned by those editors came from that small five per cent. of college educated persons. Less than four per cent. of the lawyers were college-bred, yet they furnished more than one-half of all who became successful. Not one per cent. of the business men of the country were college educated, yet that small fraction of college-bred men had seventeen times the chances of success that their fellow men of business had. In brief, the college-educated lawyer has fifty per cent. more chances for success than those not so favored; the college-educated physician, forty-six per cent. more; the author, thirty-seven per cent. more; the statesman, thirty-three per cent.; the clergy man, fifty-eight per cent.; the educator, sixty-one per cent.; the scientist, sixty-three per cent. You should therefore get the best and most complete education that it is possible for you to obtain.

Knowledge, then, is one of the secret keys which unlock the hidden mysteries of a successful life.

"I do not remember," said Beecher, "a book in all the depths of learning, nor a scrap in literature, nor a work in all the schools of art, from which its author has derived a permanent renown, that is not known to have been long and patiently elaborated."

"You are a fool to stick so close to your work all the time," said one of Vanderbilt's young friends; "we are having our fun while we are young, for when will we if not now?" But Cornelius was either earning more money by working overtime, or saving what he had earned, or at home asleep, recruiting for the next day's labor and preparing for a large harvest later. Like all successful men, he made finance a study. When he entered the railroad business, it was estimated that his fortune was thirty-five or forty million dollars.

"The spruce young spark," says Sizer, "who thinks chiefly of his mustache and boots and shiny hat, of getting along nicely and easily during the day, and talking about the theatre, the opera, or a fast horse, ridiculing the faithful young fellow who came to learn the business and make a man of himself, because he will not join in wasting his time in dissipation, will see the day, if his useless life is not earlier blasted by vicious indulgences, when he will be glad to accept a situation from his fellow-clerk whom he now ridicules and affects to despise, when the latter shall stand in the firm, dispensing benefits and acquiring fortune."

"When a man has done his work," says Ruskin, "and nothing can any way be materially altered in his fate, let him forget his toil, and jest with his fate if he will; but what excuse can you find for willfulness of thought at the very time when every crisis of fortune hangs on your decisions? A youth thoughtless, when all the happiness of his home forever depends on the chances or the passions of the hour! A youth thoughtless, when the career of all his days depends on the opportunity of a moment! A youth thoughtless, when his every action is a foundation-stone of future conduct, and every imagination a foundation of life or death! Be thoughtless in any after years, rather than now—though, indeed, there is only one place where a man may be nobly thoughtless, his deathbed. Nothing should ever be left to be done there."

"On to Berlin," was the shout of the French army in July, 1870; but, to the astonishment of the world, the French forces were cut in two and rolled as by a tidal wave into Metz and around Sedan. Soon two French armies and the Emperor surrendered, and German troopers paraded the streets of captured Paris.

But as men thought it out, as Professor Wells tells us, they came to see that it was not France that was beaten, but only Louis Napoleon and a lot of nobles, influential only because they bore titles or were favorites. Louis Napoleon, the feeble bearer of a great name, was emperor because of that name and criminal daring. By a series of happy accidents he had gained credit in the Crimean War, and at Magenta and Solferino. But the unmasking time came in the Franco-Prussian War, as it always comes when sham, artificial toy-men meet genuine self-made men. And such were the German leaders,—William, strong, upright, warlike, "every inch a king;" Von Roon, Minister of War, a master of administrative detail; Bismarck, the master mind of European politics; and, above all, Von Moltke, chief of staff, who hurled armies by telegraph, as he sat at his cabinet, as easily as a master moves chessmen against a stupid opponent.

Said Captain Bingham: "You can have no idea of the wonderful machine that the German army is and how well it is prepared for war. A chart is made out which shows just what must be done in the case of wars with the different nations. And every officer's place in the scheme is laid out beforehand. There is a schedule of trains which will supersede all other schedules the moment war is declared, and this is so arranged that the commander of the army here could telegraph to any officer to take such a train and go to such a place at a moment's notice. When the Franco-Prussian War was declared, Von Moltke was awakened at midnight and told of the fact. He said coolly to the official who aroused him, 'Go to pigeonhole No. —— in my safe and take a paper from it and telegraph as there directed to the different troops of the empire.' He then turned over and went to sleep and awoke at his usual hour in the morning. Every one else in Berlin was excited about the war, but Von Moltke took his morning walk as usual, and a friend who met him said, 'General, you seem to be taking it very easy. Aren't you afraid of the situation? I should think you would be busy.' 'Ah,' replied Von Moltke, 'all of my work for this time has been done long beforehand, and everything that can be done now has been done.'"

"A rare man this Von Moltke!" exclaims Professor Wells; "one who made himself ready for his opportunities beyond all men known to the modern world. Of an impoverished family, he rose very slowly and by his own merit. He yielded to no temptation, vice, or dishonesty, of course, nor to the greater and ever present temptation to idleness, for he constantly worked to the limit of human endurance. He was ready for every emergency, not by accident, but because he made himself ready by painstaking labor, before the opportunity came. His favorite motto was, '*Help yourself and others will help you.*' Hundreds of his age in the Prussian army were of nobler birth, thousands of greater fortune, but he made himself superior to them all by extraordinary fidelity and diligence.

"The greatest master of strategy the world has ever seen was sixty-six years at school to himself before he was ready for his task. Though born with the century, and an army officer at nineteen, he was an old man when, in 1866, as Prussian chief of staff, he crushed Austria at Sadowa and drove her out of Germany. Four years later the silent, modest soldier of seventy, ready for the still greater opportunity, smote France, and changed the map of Europe. Glory and the field-marshal's baton, after fifty-one years of hard work! No wonder Louis Napoleon was beaten by such men as he. All Louis Napoleons have been, and always will be. Opportunity always finds out frauds. It does not make men, but shows the world what they have made of themselves."

Sir Henry Havelock joined the army of India in his twenty-eighth year, and waited till he was sixty-two for the opportunity to show himself fitted to command and skillful to plan. During those four and thirty years of waiting, he was busy preparing himself for that march to Lucknow which was to make him famous as a soldier.

Farragut,

"The viking of our western climeWho made his mast a throne,"

began his naval career as a mere boy, and was sixty-four years old before he had an opportunity to distinguish himself; but when the great test of his life came, the reserve of half a century's preparation made him master of the situation.

Alexander Hamilton said, "Men give me credit for genius. All the genius I have lies just in this: when I have a subject in hand I study it profoundly. Day and night it is before me. I explore it in all its bearings. My mind becomes pervaded with it. Then the effort which I make the people are pleased to call the fruit of genius; it is the fruit of labor and thought." The law of labor is equally binding on genius and mediocrity.

"Fill up the cask! fill up the cask!" said old Dr. Bellamy when asked by a young clergyman for advice about the composition of sermons. "Fill up the cask! and then if you tap it anywhere you will get a good stream. But if you put in but little, it will dribble, dribble, dribble, and you must tap, tap, tap, and then you get but a small stream, after all."

"The merchant is in a dangerous position," says Dr. W. W. Patton, "whose means are in goods trusted out all over the country on long credits, and who in an emergency has no money in the bank upon which to draw. A heavy deposit, subject to a sight-draft, is the only position of strength. And he only is intellectually strong, who has made heavy deposits in the bank of memory, and can draw upon his faculties at any time, according to the necessities of the case."

They say that more life, if not more labor, was spent on the piles beneath the St. Petersburg church of St. Isaac's, to get a foundation, than on all the magnificent marbles and malachite which have since been lodged in it.

Fifty feet of Bunker Hill Monument is under ground, unseen, and unappreciated by the thousands who tread about that historic shaft. The rivers of India run under ground, unseen, unheard, by the millions who tramp above, but are they therefore lost? Ask the golden harvest waving above them if it feels the water flowing beneath? The superstructure of a lifetime cannot stand upon the foundation of a day.

C. H. Parkhurst says that in manhood, as much as in house-building, the foundation keeps asserting itself all the way from the first floor to the roof. The stones laid in the underpinning may be coarse and inelegant, but, even so, each such stone perpetuates itself in silent echo clear up through to the finial. The body is in that respect like an old Stradivarius violin, the ineffable sweetness of whose music is outcome and quotation from the coarse fibre of the case upon which its strings are strung. It is a very pleasant delusion that what we call the higher qualities and energies of a person maintain that self-centered kind of existence that enables them to discard and contemn all dependence upon what is lower and less refined than themselves, but it is a delusion that always wilts in an atmosphere of fact. Climb high as we like our ladder will still require to rest on the ground; and it is probable that the keenest intellectual intuition, and the most delicate throb of passion would, if analysis could be carried so far, be discovered to have its connections with the rather material affair that we know as the body.

Lincoln took the postmastership for the sake of reading all the papers that came to town. He read everything he could lay his hands on; the Bible, Shakespeare, Pilgrim's Progress, Life of Washington and Life of Franklin, Life of Henry Clay, Æsop's Fables; he read them over and over again until he could almost repeat them by heart; but he never read a novel in his life. His education came from the newspapers and from his contact with men and things. After he read a book he would write out an analysis of it. What a grand sight to see this long, lank, backwoods student, lying before the fire in a log cabin without floor or windows, after everybody else was abed, devouring books he had borrowed but could not afford to buy!

"I have been watching the careers of young men by the thousand in this busy city of New York for over thirty years," said Dr. Cuyler, "and I find that the chief difference between the successful and the failures lies in the single element of staying power. Permanent success is oftener won by holding on than by sudden dash, however brilliant. The easily discouraged, who are pushed back by a straw, are all the time dropping to the rear—to perish or to be carried along on the stretcher of charity. They who understand and practice Abraham Lincoln's homely maxim of 'pegging away' have achieved the solidest success."

It is better to deserve success than to merely have it; few deserve it who do not attain it. There is no failure in this country for those whose personal habits are good, and who follow some honest calling industriously, unselfishly, and purely. If one desires to succeed, he must pay the price, work.

No matter how weak a power may be, rational use will make it stronger. No matter how awkward your movements may be, how obtuse your senses, or how crude your thought, or how unregulated your desires, you may by patient discipline acquire, slowly indeed but with infallible certainty, grace and freedom of action, clearness and acuteness of perception, strength and precision of thought, and moderation of desire.

It would go very far to destroy the absurd and pernicious association of genius and idleness, to show that the greatest poets, orators, statesmen, and historians—men of the most imposing and brilliant talents—have actually labored as hard as the makers of dictionaries and arrangers of indexes; and the most obvious reason why they have been superior to other men, is, that they have taken more pains.

Even the great genius, Lord Bacon, left large quantities of material entitled "Sudden thoughts set down for use." John Foster was an indefatigable worker. "He used to hack, split, twist, and pull up by the roots, or practice any other severity on whatever did not please him." Chalmers was asked in London what Foster was doing. "Hard at it" he said, "at the rate of a line a week."

When a young lawyer, Daniel Webster once looked in vain through all the libraries near him, and then ordered at an expense of $50 the necessary books, to obtain authorities and precedents in a case in which his client was a poor blacksmith. He won his case, but, on account of the poverty of his client, only charged $15, thus losing heavily on the books bought, to say nothing of his time. Years after, as he was passing through New York city, he was consulted by Aaron Burr on an important but puzzling case then pending before the Supreme Court. Webster saw in a moment that it was just like the blacksmith's case, an intricate question of title, which he had solved so thoroughly that it was to him simple as the multiplication table. Going back to the time of Charles II., he gave the law and precedents involved with such readiness and accuracy of sequence that Burr asked, in great surprise: "Mr. Webster, have you been consulted before in this case?"

"Most certainly not. I never heard of your case till this evening."

"Very well," said Burr, "proceed." And when he had finished, Webster received a fee that paid him liberally for all the time and trouble he had spent for his early client.

What the age wants is men who have the nerve and the grit to work and wait, whether the world applaud or hiss. It wants a Bancroft, who can spend twenty-six years on the "History of the United States;" a Noah Webster, who can devote thirty-six years to a dictionary; a Gibbon, who can plod for twenty years on the "Decline and Fall of the Roman Empire;" a Mirabeau, who can struggle on for forty years before he has a chance to show his vast reserve, destined to shake an empire; a Farragut, a Von Moltke, who have the persistence to work and wait for half a century for their first great opportunities; a Garfield, burning his lamp fifteen minutes later than a rival student in his academy; a Grant, fighting on in heroic silence, when denounced by his brother generals and politicians everywhere; a Field's untiring perseverance, spending years and a fortune laying a cable when all the world called him a fool; a Michael Angelo, working seven long years decorating the Sistine Chapel with his matchless "Creation" and the "Last Judgment," refusing all remuneration therefor, lest his pencil might catch the taint of avarice; a Titian, spending seven years on the "Last Supper;" a Stephenson, working fifteen years on a locomotive; a Watt, twenty years on a condensing engine; a Lady Franklin, working incessantly for twelve long years to rescue her husband from the polar seas; a Thurlow Weed, walking two miles through the snow with rags tied around his feet for shoes, to borrow the history of the French Revolution, and eagerly devouring it before the sap-bush fire; a Milton, elaborating "Paradise Lost" in a world he could not see, and then selling it for fifteen pounds; a Thackeray, struggling on cheerfully after his "Vanity Fair" was refused by a dozen publishers; a Balzac, toiling and waiting in a lonely garret, whom neither poverty, debt, nor hunger could discourage or intimidate; not daunted by privations, not hindered by discouragements. It wants men who can work and wait.

That is done soon enough which is done well. Soon ripe, soon rotten. He that would enjoy the fruit must not gather the flower. He who is impatient to become his own master is more likely to become his own slave. Better believe yourself a dunce and work away than a genius and be idle. One year of trained thinking is worth more than a whole college course of mental absorption of a vast series of undigested facts. The facility with which the world swallows up the ordinary college graduate who thought he was going to dazzle mankind should bid you pause and reflect. But just as certainly as man was created not to crawl on all fours in the depths of primeval forests, but to develop his mental and moral faculties, just so certainly he needs education, and only by means of it will he become what he ought to become,—man, in the highest sense of the word. Ignorance is not simply the negation of knowledge, it is the misdirection of the mind. "One step in knowledge," says Bulwer, "is one step from sin; one step from sin is one step nearer to Heaven."

CHAPTER VIII

THE CONQUEST OF OBSTACLES

Nature, when she adds difficulties, adds brains.—EMERSON.

Exigencies create the necessary ability to meet and conquer them.—WENDELL PHILLIPS.

Many men owe the grandeur of their lives to their tremendous difficulties.—SPURGEON.

The rugged metal of the mineMust burn before its surface shine.—BYRON.

When a man looks through a tear in his own eye, that is a lens which opens reaches in the unknown, and reveals orbs no telescope could do.—BEECHER.

No man ever worked his way in a dead calm.—JOHN NEAL.

"Kites rise against, not with, the wind."

Then welcome each rebuff,That turns earth's smoothness rough,Each sting, that bids not sit nor stand, but go.—BROWNING.

"What a fine profession ours would be if there were no gibbets!" said one of two highwaymen who chanced to pass a gallows. "Tut, you blockhead," replied the other, "gibbets are the making of us; for, if there were no gibbets, every one would be a highwayman." Just so with every art, trade, or pursuit; it is the difficulties that scare and keep out unworthy competitors.

"Life," says a philosopher, "refuses to be so adjusted as to eliminate from it all strife and conflict and pain. There are a thousand tasks, that, in larger interests than ours, must be done, whether we want them or no. The world refuses to walk upon tiptoe, so that we may be able to sleep. It gets up very early and stays up very late, and all the while there is the conflict of myriads of hammers and saws and axes with the stubborn material that in no other way can be made to serve its use and do its work for man. And then, too, these hammers and axes are not wielded without strain or pang, but swung by the millions of toilers who labor with their cries and groans and tears. Nay, our temple building, whether it be for God or man, exacts its bitter toll, and fills life with cries and blows. The thousand rivalries of our daily business, the fierce animosities when we are beaten, the even fiercer exultation when we have beaten, the crashing blows of disaster, the piercing scream of defeat—these things we have not yet gotten rid of, nor in this life ever will. Why should we wish to get rid of them? We are here, my brother, to be hewed and hammered and planed in God's quarry and on God's anvil for a nobler life to come." Only the muscle that is used is developed.

"Troubles are often the tools by which God fashions us for better things," said Beecher. "Far up the mountain side lies a block of granite, and says to itself, 'How happy am I in my serenity—above the winds, above the trees, almost above the flight of birds! Here I rest, age after age, and nothing disturbs me.'

"Yet what is it? It is only a bare block of granite, jutting out of the cliff, and its happiness is the happiness of death.

"By and by comes the miner, and with strong and repeated strokes he drills a hole in its top, and the rock says, 'What does this mean?' Then the black powder is poured in, and with a blast that makes the mountain echo, the block is blown asunder, and goes crashing down into the valley. 'Ah!' it exclaims as it falls, 'why this rending?' Then come saws to cut and fashion it; and humbled now, and willing to be nothing, it is borne away from the mountain and conveyed to the city. Now it is chiseled and polished, till, at length, finished in beauty, by block and tackle it is raised, with mighty hoistings, high in air, to be the top-stone on some monument of the country's glory."

"It is this scantiness of means, this continual deficiency, this constant hitch, this perpetual struggle to keep the head above water and the wolf from the door, that keeps society from falling to pieces. Let every man have a few more dollars than he wants, and anarchy would follow."

"Do you wish to live without a trial?" asks a modern teacher. "Then you wish to die but half a man. Without trial you cannot guess at your own strength. Men do not learn to swim on a table. They must go into deep water and buffet the waves. Hardship is the native soil of manhood and self-reliance. Trials are rough teachers, but rugged schoolmasters make rugged pupils. A man who goes through life prosperous, and comes to his grave without a wrinkle, is not half a man. Difficulties are God's errands. And when we are sent upon them we should esteem it a proof of God's confidence. We should reach after the highest good."

Suddenly, with much jarring and jolting, an electric car came to a standstill just in front of a heavy truck that was headed in an opposite direction. The huge truck wheels were sliding uselessly round on the car tracks that were wet and slippery from rain. All the urging of the teamster and the straining of the horses were in vain—until the motorman quietly tossed a shovelful of sand on the track under the heavy wheels, and then the truck lumbered on its way. "Friction is a very good thing," remarked a passenger.

There is a beautiful tale of Scandinavian mythology. A hero, under the promise of becoming a demi-god, is bidden in the celestial halls to perform three test-acts of prowess. He is to drain the drinking-horn of Thor. Then he must run a race with a courser so fleet that he fairly spurns the ground under his flying footsteps. Then he must wrestle with a toothless old woman, whose sinewy hands, as wiry as eagle claws in the grapple, make his very flesh to quiver. He is victorious in them all. But as the crown of success is placed upon his temples, he discovers for the first time that he has had for his antagonist the three greatest forces of nature. He raced with thought, he wrestled with old age, he drank the sea. Nature, like the God of nature, wrestles with us as a friend, not an enemy, wanting us to gain the victory, and wrestles with us that we may understand and enjoy her best blessings. Every greatest and highest earthly good has come to us unfolded and enriched by this terrible wrestling with nature.

A curious society still exists in Paris composed of dramatic authors who meet once a month and dine together. Their number has no fixed limit, only every member to be eligible must have been hissed. An eminent dramatist is selected for chairman and holds the post for three months. His election generally follows close upon a splendid failure. Some of the world-famous ones have enjoyed this honor. Dumas, Jr., Zola and Offenbach have all filled the chair and presided at the monthly dinner. These dinners are given on the last Friday of the month, and are said to be extraordinarily hilarious.

"I do believe God wanted a grand poem of that man," said George Macdonald of Milton, "and so blinded him that he might be able to write it."

"Returned with thanks" has made many an author. Failure often leads a man to success by arousing his latent energy, by firing a dormant purpose, by awakening powers which were sleeping. Men of mettle turn disappointments into helps as the oyster turns into pearls the sand which annoys it.

"Let the adverse breath of criticism be to you only what the blast of the storm wind is to the eagle,—a force against him that lifts him higher."

"I do not see," says Emerson, "how any man can afford, for the sake of his nerves and his nap, to spare any action in which he can partake. It is pearls and rubies to his discourse. Drudgery, calamity, exasperation, want, are instructors in eloquence and wisdom. The true scholar grudges every opportunity of action passed by as a loss of power."

"Adversity is a severe instructor," says Edmund Burke, "set over us by one who knows us better than we do ourselves, as He loves us better too. He that wrestles with us strengthens our nerves and sharpens our skill. Our antagonist is our helper. This conflict with difficulty makes us acquainted with our object, and compels us to consider it in all its relations. It will not suffer us to be superficial."

Strong characters, like the palm tree, seem to thrive best when most abused. Men who have stood up bravely under great misfortune for years are often unable to bear prosperity. Their good fortune takes the spring out of their energy, as the torrid zone enervates races accustomed to a vigorous climate. Some people never come to themselves until baffled, rebuffed, thwarted, defeated, crushed, in the opinion of those around them. Trials unlock their virtues; defeat is the threshold of their victory.

"Every man who makes a fortune has been more than once a bankrupt, if the truth were known," said Albion Tourgée. "Grant's failure as a subaltern made him commander-in-chief, and for myself, my failure to accomplish what I set out to do led me to what I never had aspired to."

"What is defeat?" asked Wendell Phillips. "Nothing but education." And a life's disaster may become the landmark from which there has begun a new era, a broader life for man.

"To make his way at the bar," said an eminent jurist, "a young man must live like a hermit and work like a horse. There is nothing that does a young lawyer so much good as to be half starved."

We are the victors of our opponents. They have developed in us the very power by which we overcome them. Without their opposition we could never have braced and anchored and fortified ourselves, as the oak is braced and anchored for its thousand battles with the tempests. Our trials, our sorrows, and our griefs develop us in a similar way.

"Obstacles," says Mitchell, "are great incentives. I lived for whole years upon Virgil and found myself well off." Poverty, Horace tells us, drove him to poetry.

Nothing more unmans a man than to take away from him the spur of necessity, which urges him onward and upward to the goal of his ambition. Man is naturally lazy, and wealth induces indolence. The great object of life is development, the unfolding and drawing out of our powers, and whatever tempts us to a life of indolence or inaction, or to seek pleasure merely, whatever furnishes us a crutch when we can develop our muscles better by walking, all helps, guides, props, whatever tempts to a life of inaction, in whatever guise it may come, is a curse. I always pity the boy or girl with inherited wealth, for the temptation to hide their talents in a napkin, undeveloped, is very, very great. It is not natural for them to walk when they can ride, to go alone when they can be helped.

Quentin Matsys was a blacksmith at Antwerp. When in his twentieth year he wished to marry the daughter of a painter. The father refused his consent. "Wert thou a painter," said he, "she should be thine; but a blacksmith—never!" "*I will be* a painter," said the young man. He applied to his new art with so much perseverance that in a short time he produced pictures which gave a promise of the highest excellence. He gained for his reward the fair hand for which he sighed, and rose ere long to a high rank in his profession.

Take two acorns from the same tree, as nearly alike as possible; plant one on a hill by itself, and the other in the dense forest, and watch them grow. The oak standing alone is exposed to every storm. Its roots reach out in every direction, clutching the rocks and piercing deep into the earth. Every rootlet lends itself to steady the growing giant, as if in anticipation of fierce conflict with the elements. Sometimes its upward growth seems checked for years, but all the while it has been expending its energy in pushing a root across a large rock to gain a firmer anchorage. Then it shoots proudly aloft again, prepared to defy the hurricane. The gales which sport so rudely with its wide branches find more than their match, and only serve still further to toughen every minutest fibre from pith to bark.

The acorn planted in the deep forest shoots up a weak, slender sapling. Shielded by its neighbors, it feels no need of spreading its roots far and wide for support.

Take two boys, as nearly alike as possible. Place one in the country away from the hothouse culture and refinements of the city, with only the district school, the Sunday school, and a few books. Remove wealth and props of every kind; and, if he has the right kind of material in him, he will thrive. Every obstacle overcome lends him strength for the next conflict. If he falls, he rises with more determination than before. Like a rubber ball, the harder the obstacle he meets the higher he rebounds. Obstacles and opposition are but apparatus of the gymnasium in which the fibres of his manhood are developed. He compels respect and recognition from those who have ridiculed his poverty. Put the other boy in a Vanderbilt family. Give him French and German nurses; gratify every wish. Place him under the tutelage of great masters and send him to Harvard. Give him thousands a year for spending money, and let him travel extensively.

The two meet. The city lad is ashamed of his country brother. The plain, threadbare clothes, hard hands, tawny face, and awkward manner of the country boy make sorry contrast with the genteel appearance of the other. The poor boy bemoans his hard lot, regrets that he has "no chance in life," and envies the city youth. He thinks that it is a cruel Providence that places such a wide gulf between them. They meet again as men, but how changed! It is as easy to distinguish the sturdy, self-made man from the one who has been propped up all his life by wealth, position, and family influence, as it is for the shipbuilder to tell the difference between the plank from the rugged mountain oak and one from the sapling of the forest. If you think there is no difference, place each plank in the bottom of a ship, and test them in a hurricane at sea.

The athlete does not carry the gymnasium away with him, but he carries the skill and muscle which give him his reputation.

The lessons you learn at school will give you strength and skill in after life, and power, just in proportion to the accuracy, the clearness of perception with which you learn your lessons. The school was your gymnasium. You do not carry away the Greek and Latin text-books, the geometry and algebra into your occupations any more than the athlete carries the apparatus of the gymnasium, but you carry away the skill and the power if you have been painstaking, accurate and faithful.

"It is in me, and it *shall* come out!" And it did. For Richard Brinsley Sheridan became the most brilliant, eloquent and amazing statesman of his day. Yet if his first efforts had been but moderately successful, he might have been content with mere mediocrity. It was his defeats that nerved him to strive for eminence and win it. But it took hard, persistent work in his case to secure it, just as it did in that of so many others.

Byron was stung into a determination to go to the top by a scathing criticism of his first book, "Hours of Idleness," published when he was but nineteen years of age. Macaulay said, "There is scarce an instance in history of so sudden a rise to so dizzy an eminence as Byron reached." In a few years he stood by the side of such men as Scott, Southey and Campbell. Many an orator like "stuttering Jack Curran," or "Orator Mum," as he was once called, has been spurred into eloquence by ridicule and abuse.

Where the sky is gray and the climate unkindly, where the soil yields nothing save to the diligent hand, and life itself cannot be supported without incessant toil, man has reached his highest range of physical and intellectual development.

The most beautiful and the strongest animals, as a rule, have come from the same narrow belt of latitude which has produced the heroes of the world.

The most beautiful as well as the strongest characters are not developed in warm climates, where man finds his bread ready made on trees, and where exertion is a great effort, but rather in a trying climate and on a stubborn soil. It is no chance that returns to the Hindoo ryot a penny and to the American laborer a dollar for his daily toil; that makes Mexico with her mineral wealth poor, and New England with its granite and ice rich. It is rugged necessity, it is the struggle to obtain, it is poverty the priceless spur, that develops the stamina of manhood, and calls the race out of barbarism. Labor found the world a wilderness and has made it a garden.

The law of adaptation by which conditions affect an organism is simple and well known. It is that which callouses the palm of the oarsman, strengthens the waist of the wrestler, fits the back to its burden. It inexorably compels the organism to adapt itself to its conditions, to like them, and so to survive them.

As soon as young eagles can fly the old birds tumble them out and tear the down and feathers from their nest. The rude and rough experience of the eaglet fits him to become the bold king of birds, fierce and expert in pursuing his prey.

Benjamin Franklin ran away and George Law was turned out of doors. Thrown upon their own resources, they early acquired the energy and skill to overcome difficulties.

Boys who are bound out, crowded out, kicked out, usually "turn out," while those who do not have these disadvantages frequently fail to "come out."

From an aimless, idle and useless brain, emergencies often call out powers and virtues before unknown and unsuspected. How often we see a young man develop astounding ability and energy after the death of a parent or the loss of a fortune, or after some other calamity has knocked the props and crutches from under him. The prison has roused the slumbering fire in many a noble mind. "Robinson Crusoe" was written in prison. The "Pilgrim's Progress" appeared in Bedford Jail. The "Life and Times" of Baxter, Eliot's "Monarchia of Man," and Penn's "No Cross, No Crown," were written by prisoners. Sir Walter Raleigh wrote "The History of the World" during his imprisonment of thirteen years. Luther translated the Bible while confined in the Castle of Wartburg. For twenty years Dante worked in exile, and even under sentence of death. His works were burned in public after his death; but genius will not burn.

Adversity exasperates fools, dejects cowards, draws out the faculties of the wise and industrious, puts the modest to the necessity of trying their skill, awes the opulent, and makes the idle industrious. Neither do uninterrupted success and prosperity qualify men for usefulness and happiness. The storms of adversity, like those of the ocean, rouse the faculties, and excite the invention, prudence, skill and fortitude of the voyager. The martyrs of ancient times, in bracing their minds to outward calamities, acquired a loftiness of purpose and a moral heroism worth a lifetime of softness and security. A man upon whom continuous sunshine falls is like the earth in August: he becomes parched and dry and hard and close-grained. Men have drawn from adversity the elements of greatness. If you have the blues, go and see the poorest and sickest families within your knowledge. The darker the setting, the brighter the diamond. Don't run about and tell acquaintances that you have been unfortunate; people do not like to have unfortunate men for acquaintances.

This is the crutch age. "Helps" and "aids" are advertised everywhere. We have institutes, colleges, universities, teachers, books, libraries, newspapers, magazines. Our thinking is done for us. Our problems are all worked out in "explanations" and "keys." Our boys are too often tutored through college with very little study. "Short roads" and "abridged methods" are characteristic of the century. Ingenious methods are used everywhere to get the drudgery out of the college course. Newspapers give us our politics, and preachers our religion. Self-help and self-reliance are getting old fashioned. Nature, as if conscious of delayed blessings, has rushed to man's relief with her wondrous forces, and undertakes to do the world's drudgery and emancipate him from Eden's curse.

CHAPTER IX

DEAD IN EARNEST

It is the live coal that kindles others, not the dead. What made Demosthenes the greatest of all orators was that he appeared the most entirely possessed by the feelings he wished to inspire. The effect produced by Charles Fox, who by the exaggerations of party spirit, was often compared to Demosthenes, seems to have arisen wholly from this earnestness, which made up for the want of almost every grace, both of manner and style.—ANON.

Twelve poor men taken out of boats and creeks, without any help of learning, should conquer the world to the cross.—STEPHEN CARNOCK.

For his heart was in his work, and the heartGiveth grace unto every art.—LONGFELLOW.

He did it with all his heart and prospered.—II. CHRONICLES.

The only conclusive evidence of a man's sincerity is that he gives himself for a principle. Words, money, all things else are comparatively easy to give away; but when a man makes a gift of his daily life and practice, it is plain that the truth, whatever it may be, has taken possession of him.—LOWELL.

"The emotions," says Whipple, "may all be included in the single word 'enthusiasm,' or that impulsive force which liberates the mental power from the ice of timidity as spring loosens the streams from the grasp of winter, and sends them forth in a rejoicing rush. The mind of youth, when impelled by this original strength and enthusiasm of Nature, is keen, eager, inquisitive, intense, audacious, rapidly assimilating facts into faculties and knowledge into power, and above all teeming with that joyous fullness of creative life which radiates thoughts as inspirations, and magnetizes as well as informs."

"Columbus, my hero," exclaims Carlyle, "royalist sea-king of all! It is no friendly environment this of thine, in the waste, deep waters; around thee mutinous discouraged souls, behind thee disgrace and ruin, before thee the unpenetrated veil of night. Brother, these wild water-mountains, bounding from their deep bases (ten miles deep, I am told), are not there on thy behalf! Meseems *they* have other work than floating thee forward:—and the huge winds, that sweep from Ursa Major to the tropics and equator, dancing their giant-waltz through the kingdoms of chaos and immensity, they care little about filling rightly or filling wrongly the small shoulder-of-mutton sails in this cockle skiff of thine! Thou art not among articulate-speaking friends, my brother; thou art among immeasurable dumb monsters, tumbling, howling wide as the world here. Secret, far-off, invisible to all hearts but thine, there lies a help in them: see how thou wilt get at that. Patiently thou wilt wait till the mad southwester spend itself, saving thyself by dexterous science of defence the while: valiantly, with swift decision, wilt thou strike in, when the favoring east wind, the possible, springs up. Mutiny of men thou wilt sternly repress; weakness, despondency, thou wilt cheerily encourage: thou wilt swallow down complaint, unreason, weariness, weakness of others and thyself;—how much wilt thou swallow down? There shall be a depth of silence in thee, deeper than this sea, which is but ten miles deep: a silence unsoundable; known to God only. Thou shalt be a great man. Yes, my world-soldier, thou of the world marine-service,—thou wilt have to be greater than this tumultuous unmeasured world here round thee is: thou, in thy strong soul, as with wrestler's arms, shall embrace it, harness it down; and make it bear thee on,—to new Americas, or whither God wills!"

With what concentration of purpose did Washington put the whole weight of his character into the scales of our cause in the Revolution! With what earnest singleness of aim did Lincoln in the cabinet, Grant in the field, throw his whole soul into the contest of our civil war?

The power of Phillips Brooks, at which men wondered, lay in his tremendous earnestness.

"No matter what your work is," says Emerson, "let it be yours; no matter if you are a tinker or preacher, blacksmith or president, let what you are doing be organic, let it be in your bones, and you open the door by which the affluence of heaven and earth shall stream into you." Again, he says: "God will not have His works made manifest by cowards. A man is relieved and gay when he has put his heart into his work and done his best; but what he has said or done otherwise, shall give him no peace. It is a deliverance which does not deliver. In the attempt, his genius deserts him; no muse befriends; no invention, no hope."

"I do not know how it is with others when speaking on an important question," said Henry Clay; "but on such occasions I seem to be unconscious of the external world. Wholly engrossed by the subject before me, I lose all sense of personal identity, of time, or of surrounding objects."

"I have been so busy for twenty years trying to save the souls of other people," said Livingstone, "that I had forgotten that I have one of my own until a savage auditor asked me if I felt the influence of the religion I was advocating."

"Well, I've worked hard enough for it," said Malibran when a critic expressed his admiration of her D in alt, reached by running up three octaves from low D; "I've been chasing it for a month. I pursued it everywhere,—when I was dressing, when I was doing my hair; and at last I found it on the toe of a shoe that I was putting on."

"People smile at the enthusiasm of youth," said Charles Kingsley; "that enthusiasm which they themselves secretly look back at with a sigh, perhaps unconscious that it is partly their own fault that they ever lost it."

"Should I die this minute," said Nelson at an important crisis, "want of frigates would be found written on my heart."

Said Dr. Arnold, the celebrated instructor: "I feel more and more the need of intercourse with men who take life in earnest. It is painful to me to be always on the surface of things. Not that I wish for much of what is called religious conversation. That is often apt to be on the surface. But I want a sign which one catches by a sort of masonry, that a man knows what he is about in life. When I find this it opens my heart with as fresh a sympathy as when I was twenty years younger."

Archimedes, the greatest geometer of antiquity, was consulted by the king in regard to a gold crown suspected of being fraudulently alloyed with silver. While considering the best method of detecting any fraud, he plunged into a full bathing tub; and, with the thought that the water that overflowed must be equal in weight to his body, he discovered the method of obtaining the bulk of the crown compared with an equally heavy mass of pure gold. Excited by the discovery, he ran through the streets undressed, crying, "I have found it."

Equally celebrated is his remark, "Give me where to stand and I will move the world."

His only remark to the Roman soldier who entered his room while engaged in geometrical study, was, "Don't step on my circle."

Refusing to follow the soldier to Marcellus, who had captured the city, he was killed on the spot. He is said to have remarked, "My head, but not my circle."

"Every great and commanding moment in the annals of the world," says Emerson, "is the triumph of some enthusiasm. The victories of the Arabs after Mahomet, who, in a few years, from a small and mean beginning, established a larger empire than that of Rome, is an example. They did they knew not what. The naked Derar, horsed on an idea, was found an overmatch for a troop of cavalry. The women fought like men and conquered the Roman men. They were miserably equipped, miserably fed. They were temperance troops. There was neither brandy nor flesh needed to feed them. They conquered Asia and Africa and Spain on barley. The Caliph Omar's walking-stick struck more terror into those who saw it than another man's sword."

Horace Vernet's enthusiasm and devotion to the one idea of his life knew no bounds. He had himself lashed to the mast in a terrible gale on the Mediterranean when all others on board were seized with terror, and with great delight sketched the towering waves which threatened every minute to swallow the vessel. Several writers tell the story that a great artist, Giotto, about to paint the crucifixion, induced a poor man to let him bind him upon a cross in order that he might get a better idea of the terrible scene that he was about to put upon the canvas. He promised faithfully that he would release his model in an hour, but to the latter's horror the painter seized a dagger and plunged it into his heart; and, while the blood was streaming from the ghastly wound, painted his death agony.

Beecher was a very dull boy and was the last member of the family of whom anything was expected. He had a weak memory, and disliked study. He shunned society and wanted to go to sea. Even when he went to college many of his classmates stood ahead of him, who have fallen into oblivion. But when he was converted his whole life changed: he was full of enthusiasm, hopefulness and zeal. Nothing was too menial for him to undertake to carry his purpose. He chopped wood, built the fire in his little church in Lawrenceburg, Ind., of only eighteen members, cleaned the lamps, swept the floor and washed the windows. He built the fire, baked, washed, when his wife was ill. The pent-up enthusiasm of his ambitious life burst the barriers of his inhospitable surroundings until he blossomed out into America's greatest pulpit orator.

When Handel was a little boy he bought a clavichord, hid it in the attic, and went there at night to play upon it, muffling the strings with small pieces of fine woolen cloth so that the sounds should not wake the family. Michael Angelo neglected school to copy drawings which he dared not carry home. Murillo filled the margin of his school-book with drawings. Dryden read Polybius before he was ten years old. Le Brum, when a boy, drew with a piece of charcoal on the walls of the house. Pope wrote excellent verses at fourteen. Blaise Pascal, the French mathematician, composed at sixteen a tract on the conic sections.

Professor Agassiz was so enthusiastic in his work and so loved the fishes, the fowl and the cattle that it is said these creatures would die for him to give him their skeletons. His father wanted him to fit for commercial life, but the fish haunted him day and night.

Confucius said that "he was so eager in the pursuit of knowledge that he forgot his food;" and that, "in the joy of its attainment, he forgot his sorrows;" and that "he did not even perceive that old age was coming on."

"That boy tries to make himself useful," said an employer of the errand boy, George W. Childs. It is this trying to be useful and helpful that promotes us in life.

Once, when Mr. Harvey, an accomplished mathematician, was in a bookseller's shop, he saw a poor lad of mean appearance enter and write something on a slip of paper and give it to the proprietor. On inquiry he found this was a poor deaf boy, Kitto, who afterward became one of the most noted Biblical scholars in the world, and who wrote his first book in the poor-house. He had come to borrow a book. When a lad he had fallen backward from a ladder thirty-five feet upon the pavement with a load of slates that he was carrying to the roof. The poor lad was so thirsty for books that he would borrow from booksellers who would loan them to him out of pity, read them and return them.

The *Youth's Companion* says that Mr. Edison in his new biography—his "Life and Inventions"—describes the accidental method by which he discovered the principle of the phonograph. There is a kind of accident that happens only to a certain kind of man.

"I was singing to the mouthpiece of a telephone," Mr. Edison says, "when the vibrations of the voice sent the fine steel point into my finger. That set me to thinking. If I could record the actions of the point, and send the point over the same surface afterward, I saw no reason why the thing would not talk.

"I tried the experiment first on a slip of telegraph paper and found that the point made an alphabet. I shouted the words 'Halloo! Halloo!' into the mouthpiece, ran the paper back over the steel point, and heard a faint 'Halloo! Halloo!' in return.

"I determined to make a machine that would work accurately, and gave my assistants instructions, telling them what I had discovered. They laughed at me. That's the whole story. The phonograph is the result of the pricking of a finger."

It is one thing to hit upon an idea, however, and another thing to carry it out to perfection. The machine would talk, but, like many young children, it had difficulty with certain sounds—in the present case with aspirants and sibilants. Mr. Edison's biographers say, but the statement is somewhat exaggerated:

"He has frequently spent from fifteen to twenty hours daily, for six or seven months on a stretch, dinning the word 'Spezia,' for example, into the stubborn surface of the wax. 'Spezia,' roared the inventor, 'Pezia' lisped the phonograph in tones of ladylike reserve, and so on through thousands of graded repetitions till the desired results were obtained.

"The primary education of the phonograph was comical in the extreme. To hear those grave and reverend signors, rich in scientific honors, patiently reiterating:

Mary had a little lamb,A little lamb, *lamb*, LAMB,

and elaborating that point with anxious gravity, was to receive a practical demonstration of the eternal unfitness of things."

Milton, when blind, old and poor, showed a royal cheerfulness and never "bated one jot of heart or hope, but steered right onward."

Dickens' characters seemed to possess him, and haunt him day and night until properly portrayed in his stories.

At a time when it was considered dangerous to society in Europe for the common people to read books and listen to lectures on any but religious subjects, Charles Knight determined to enlighten the masses by cheap literature. He believed that a paper could be instructive and not be dull, cheap without being wicked. He started the *Penny Magazine*, which acquired a circulation of 200,000 the first year. Knight projected the *Penny Cyclopedia*, the *Library of Entertaining Knowledge, Half-Hours With the Best Authors*, and other useful books at a low price. His whole adult life was spent in the work of elevating the common people by cheap, yet wholesome, publications. He died in poverty, but grateful people have erected a noble monument over his ashes.

Demosthenes roused the torpid spirits of his countrymen to a vigorous effort to preserve their independence against the designs of an ambitious and artful prince, and Philip had just reason to say he was more afraid of that man than of all the fleets and armies of the Athenians.

Horace Greeley was a hampered genius who never had a chance to show himself until he started the *Tribune*, into which he poured his whole individuality, life and soul.

Emerson lost the first years of his life trying to be somebody else. He finally came to himself and said: "If a single man plant himself indomitably on his instincts, and there abide, the whole world will come round to him in the end." "Though we travel the world over to find the beautiful we must carry it with us or we find it not." "The man that stands by himself the universe stands by him also." "Take Michael Angelo's course, 'to confide in one's self and be something of worth and value.'" "None of us will ever accomplish anything excellent or commanding except when he listens to this whisper which is heard by him alone."

Many unknown writers would make fame and fortune if, like Bunyan and Milton and Dickens and George Eliot and Scott and Emerson, they would write their own lives in their MSS., if they would write about things they have seen, that they have felt, that they have known. It is life thoughts that stir and convince, that move and persuade, that carry their very iron particles into the blood. The real heaven has never been outdone by the ideal.

Neither poverty nor misfortune could keep Linnæus from his botany.

The English and Austrian armies called Napoleon the one-hundred-thousand-man. His presence was considered equal to that force in battle.

The lesson he teaches is that which vigor always teaches—that there is always room for it. To what heaps of cowardly doubts is not that man's life an answer.

CHAPTER X

TO BE GREAT, CONCENTRATE

Let every one ascertain his special business and calling, and then stick to it.—FRANKLIN.

"He who follows two hares is sure to catch neither."

None sends his arrow to the mark in view,Whose hand is feeble, or his aim untrue.—COWPER.

He who wishes to fulfill his mission must be a man of one idea, that is, of one great overmastering purpose, overshadowing all his aims, and guiding and controlling his entire life.—BATE.

The shortest way to do anything is to do only one thing at a time.—CECIL.

The power of concentration is one of the most valuable of intellectual attainments.—HORACE MANN.

The power of a man increases steadily by continuance in one direction.—EMERSON.

Careful attention to one thing often proves superior to genius and art.—CICERO.

"It puffed like a locomotive," said a boy of the donkey engine; "it whistled like the steam-cars, but it didn't go anywhere."

The world is full of donkey-engines, of people who can whistle and puff and pull, but they don't go anywhere, they have no definite aim, no controlling purpose.

The great secret of Napoleon's power lay in his marvelous ability to concentrate his forces upon a single point. After finding the weak place in the enemy's ranks he would mass his men and hurl them upon the enemy like an avalanche until he made a breach. What a lesson of the power of concentration there is in that man's life! He was such a master of himself that he could concentrate his powers upon the smallest detail as well as upon an empire.

When Napoleon had anything to say he always went straight to his mark. He had a purpose in everything he did; there was no dilly-dallying nor shilly-shallying; he knew what he wanted to say, and said it. It was the same with all his plans; what he wanted to do, he did. He always hit the bull's eye. His great success in war was due largely to his definiteness of aim. He knew what he wanted to do, and did it. He was like a great burning glass, concentrating the rays of the sun upon a single spot; he burned a hole wherever he went.

The sun's rays scattered do no execution, but concentrated in a burning glass, they melt solid granite; yes, a diamond, even. There are plenty of men who have ability enough, the rays of their faculties taken separately are all right; but they are powerless to collect them, to concentrate them upon a single object. They lack the burning glass of a purpose, to focalize upon one spot the separate rays of their ability. Versatile men, universal geniuses, are usually weak, because they have no power to concentrate the rays of their ability, to focalize them upon one point, until they burn a hole in whatever they undertake.

This power to bring all of one's scattered forces into one focal point makes all the difference between success and failure. The sun might blaze out upon the earth forever without burning a hole in it or setting anything on fire; whereas a very few of these rays concentrated in a burning glass would, as stated, transform a diamond into vapor.

Sir James Mackintosh was a man of marvelous ability. He excited in everybody who knew him great expectations, but there was no purpose in his life to act as a burning glass to collect the brilliant rays of his intellect, by which he might have dazzled the world. Most men have ability enough, if they could only focalize it into one grand, central, all-absorbing purpose, to accomplish great things.

"To encourage me in my efforts to cultivate the power of attention," said a friend of John C. Calhoun, "he stated that to this end he had early subjected his mind to such a rigid course of discipline, and had persisted without faltering until he had acquired a perfect control over it; that he could now confine it to any subject as long as he pleased, without wandering even for a moment; that it was his uniform habit, when he set out alone to walk or ride, to select a subject for reflection, and that he never suffered his attention to wander from it until he was satisfied with its examination."

"My friend laughs at me because I have but one idea," said a learned American chemist; "but I have learned that if I wish ever to make a breach in a wall, I must play my guns continually upon one point."

"It is his will that has made him what he is," said an intimate friend of Philip D. Armour, the Chicago millionaire. "He fixes his eye on something ahead, and no matter what rises upon the right or the left he never sees it. He goes straight in pursuit of the object ahead, and overtakes it at last. He never gives up what he undertakes."

While Horace Greeley would devote a column of the New York *Tribune* to an article, Thurlow Weed would treat the same subject in a few words in the

Albany *Evening Journal,* and put the argument into such shape as to carry far more conviction.

"If you would be pungent," says Southey, "be brief; for it is with words as with sunbeams—the more they are condensed the deeper they burn."

"The only valuable kind of study," said Sydney Smith, "is to read so heartily that dinner-time comes two hours before you expected it; to sit with your Livy before you and hear the geese cackling that saved the Capitol, and to see with your own eyes the Carthaginian sutlers gathering up the rings of the Roman knights after the battle of Cannæ, and heaping them into bushels, and to be so intimately present at the actions you are reading of, that when anybody knocks at the door it will take you two or three seconds to determine whether you are in your own study or on the plains of Lombardy, looking at Hannibal's weather-beaten face and admiring the splendor of his single eye."

"Never study on speculation," says Waters; "all such study is vain. Form a plan; have an object; then work for it; learn all you can about it, and you will be sure to succeed. What I mean by studying on speculation is that aimless learning of things because they may be useful some day; which is like the conduct of the woman who bought at auction a brass door-plate with the name of Thompson on it, thinking it might be useful some day!"

"I resolved, when I began to read law," said Edward Sugden, afterward Lord St. Leonard, "to make everything I acquired perfectly my own, and never go on to a second reading till I had entirely accomplished the first. Many of the competitors read as much in a day as I did in a week; but at the end of twelve months my knowl edge was as fresh as on the day it was acquired, while theirs had glided away from their recollection."

"Very often," says Sidney Smith, "the modern precept of education is, 'Be ignorant of nothing.' But my advice is, have the courage to be ignorant of a great number of things, that you may avoid the calamity of being ignorant of all things."

"Lord, help me to take fewer things into my hands, and to do them well," is a prayer recommended by Paxton Hood to an overworked man.

"Many persons seeing me so much engaged in active life," said Edward Bulwer Lytton, "and as much about the world as if I had never been a student, have said to me, 'When do you get time to write all your books? How on earth do you contrive to do so much work?' I shall surprise you by the answer I made. The answer is this—I contrive to do so much work by never doing too much at a time. A man to get through work well must not overwork himself; or, if he do too much to-day, the reaction of fatigue will come, and he will be obliged to do too little to-morrow. Now, since I began really and earnestly to study, which was not till I had left college, and was actually in the world, I may perhaps say that I have gone through as large a course of general reading as most men of my time. I have traveled much and I have seen much; I have mixed much in politics, and in the various business of life; and in addition to all this, I have published somewhere about sixty volumes, some upon subjects requiring much special research. And what time do you think, as a general rule, I have devoted to study, to reading, and writing? Not more than three hours a day; and, when Parliament is sitting, not always that. But then, during these three hours, I have given my whole attention to what I was about."

"The things that are crowded out of a life are the test of that life. Not what we would like, but what we long for and strive for with all our might we attain."

"One great cause of failure of young men in business," says Carnegie, "is lack of concentration. They are prone to seek outside investments. The cause of many a surprising failure lies in so doing. Every dollar of capital and credit, every business-thought, should be concentrated upon the one business upon which a man has embarked. He should never scatter his shot. It is a poor business which will not yield better returns for increased capital than any outside investment. No man or set of men or corporation can manage a business-man's capital as well as he can manage it himself. The rule, 'Do not put all your eggs in one basket,' does not apply to a man's life-work. Put all your eggs in one basket and then watch that basket, is the true doctrine—the most valuable rule of all."

"A man must not only desire to be right," said Beecher, "he must *be* right. You may say, 'I wish to send this ball so as to kill the lion crouching yonder, ready to spring upon me. My wishes are all right, and I hope Providence will direct the ball.' Providence won't. You must do it; and if you do not, you are a dead man."

The ruling idea of Milton's life and the key to his mental history is his resolve to produce a great poem. Not that the aspiration in itself is singular, for it is probably shared in by every poet in his turn. As every clever schoolboy is destined by himself or his friends to become Lord-Chancellor, and every private in the French army carries in his haversack the baton of a marshal, so it is a necessary ingredient of the dream of Parnassus that it should embody itself in a form of surpassing brilliance. What distinguishes Milton from the crowd of youthful literary aspirants, *audax juventa*, is his constancy of resolve. He not only nourished through manhood the dream of youth, keeping under the importunate instincts which carry off most ambitions in middle life into the pursuit of place, profit, honor—the thorns which spring up and smother the wheat—but carried out his dream in its integrity in old age. He formed himself for this achievement and no other. Study at home, travel abroad, the arena of political controversy, the public service, the practice of the domestic virtues, were so many parts of the schooling which was to make a poet.

Bismarck adopted it as the aim of his public life "to snatch Germany from Austrian oppression," and to gather round Prussia, in a North German Confederation, all the states whose tone of thought, religion, manners and interest "were in harmony with those of Prussia." "To attain this end," he once said in conversation, "I would brave all dangers—exile, the scaffold itself. What matter if they hang me, provided the rope with which I am hung binds this new Germany firmly to the Prussian throne?"

It is related of Greeley that, when he was writing his "American Conflict," he found it necessary to conceal himself somewhere, to prevent constant interruptions. He accordingly took a room in the Bible house, where he worked from ten in the morning till five in the afternoon, and then appeared in the sanctum, seemingly as fresh as ever.

Cooper Institute is the evening school which Peter Cooper, as long ago as 1810, resolved to found some day, when he was looking about as an apprentice for a place where he could go to school evenings. Through all his career in various branches of business he never lost sight of this object; and, as his wealth increased, he was pleased that it brought nearer the realization of his dream.

"See a great lawyer like Rufus Choate," says Dr. Storrs, "in a case where his convictions are strong and his feelings are enlisted. He saw long ago, as he glanced over the box, that five of those in it were sympathetic with him; as he went on he became equally certain of seven; the number now has risen to ten; but two are still left whom he feels that he has not persuaded or mastered. Upon them he now concentrates his power, summing up the facts, setting forth anew and more forcibly the principles, urging upon them his view of the case with a more and more intense action of his mind upon theirs, until one only is left. Like the blow of a hammer, continually repeated until the iron bar crumbles beneath it, his whole force comes with ceaseless percussion on that one mind till it has yielded, and accepts the conviction on which the pleader's purpose is fixed. Men say afterward, 'He surpassed himself.' It was only because the singleness of his aim gave unity, intensity, and overpowering energy to the mind."

"The foreman of the jury, however," said Whipple, "was a hard-hearted, practical man, a model of business intellect and integrity, but with an incapacity of understanding any intellect or conscience radically differing from his own. Mr. Choate's argument, as far as the facts and the law were concerned, was through in an hour. Still he went on speaking. Hour after hour passed, and yet he continued to speak with constantly increasing eloquence, repeating and recapitulating, without any seeming reason, facts which he had already stated and arguments which he had already urged. The truth was, as I gradually learned, that he was engaged in a hand-to-hand—or rather in a brain-to-brain and a heart-to-heart—contest with the foreman, whose resistance he was determined to break down, but who confronted him for three hours with defiance observable in every rigid line of his honest countenance. 'You fool!' was the burden of the advocate's ingenious argument. 'You rascal!' was the phrase legibly printed on the foreman's incredulous face. But at last the features of the foreman began to relax, and at the end the stern lines melted into acquiescence with the opinion of the advocate, who had been storming at the defences of his mind, his heart, and his conscience for five hours, and had now entered as victor. The verdict was 'Not guilty.'"

"He who would do some great thing in this short life must apply himself to the work with such a concentration of his forces as, to idle spectators, who live only to amuse themselves, looks like insanity."

It is generally thought that when a man is said to be dissipated in his habits he must be a drinking man, or a gambler, or licentious, or all three; but dissipation is of two kinds, coarse and refined. A man can dissipate or scatter all of his mental energies and physical power by indulging in too many respectable diversions, as easily as in habits of a viler nature. Property and its cares make some men dissipated; too many friends make others. The exactions of "society," the balls, parties, receptions, and various entertainments constantly being given and attended by the *beau monde*, constitute a most wasting species of dissipation. Others, again, fritter away all their time and strength in political agitations, or in controversies and gossip; others in idling with music or some other one of the fine arts; others in feasting or fasting, as their dispositions and feelings incline. But the man of concentration of purpose is never a dissipated man in any sense, good or bad. He has no time to devote to useless trifling of any kind, but puts in as many strokes of faithful work as possible toward the attainment of some definite good.

CHAPTER XI

AT ONCE

Note the sublime precision that leads the earth over a circuit of 500,000,000 miles back to the solstice at the appointed moment without the loss of one second—no, not the millionth part of a second—for ages and ages of which it traveled that imperial road.—EDWARD EVERETT.

Despatch is the soul of business.—CHESTERFIELD.

Unfaithfulness in the keeping of an appointment is an act of clear dishonesty. You may as well borrow a person's money as his time.—HORACE MANN.

By the street of by-and-by one arrives at the house of never.—CERVANTES.

The greatest thief this world has ever produced is procrastination, and he is still at large.—H. W. SHAW.

"Oh, how I do appreciate a boy who is always on time!" says H. C. Bowen. "How quickly you learn to depend on him, and how soon you find yourself intrusting him with weightier matters! The boy who has acquired a reputation for punctuality has made the first contribution to the capital that in after years makes his success a certainty!"

"Nothing commends a young man so much to his employers," says John Stuart Blackie, "as accuracy and punctuality in the conduct of his business. And no wonder. On each man's exactitude depends the comfortable and easy going of his machine. If the clock goes fitfully nobody knows the time of day; and, if your task is a link in the chain of another man's work, you are his clock, and he ought to be able to rely on you."

"The whole period of youth," said Ruskin, "is one essentially of formation, edification, instruction. There is not an hour of it but is trembling with destinies—not a moment of which, once passed, the appointed work can ever be done again, or the neglected blow struck on the cold iron."

"To-morrow, didst thou say?" asked Cotton. "Go to—I will not hear of it. To-morrow! 't is a sharper who stakes his penury against thy plenty—who takes thy ready cash and pays thee naught but wishes, hopes and promises, the currency of idiots. *To-morrow!* it is a period nowhere to be found in all the hoary registers of time, unless perchance in the fool's calendar. Wisdom disclaims the word, nor holds society with those that own it. 'Tis fancy's child, and folly is its father; wrought of such stuffs as dreams are; and baseless as the fantastic visions of the evening." Oh, how many a wreck on the road to success could say: "I have spent all my life in the pursuit of to-morrow, being assured that to-morrow has some vast benefit or other in store for me."

"I give it as my deliberate and solemn conviction," said Dr. Fitch, "that the individual who is tardy in meeting an appointment will never be respected or successful in life."

"If a man has no regard for the time of other men," said Horace Greeley, "why should he have for their money? What is the difference between taking a man's hour and taking his five dollars? There are many men to whom each hour of the business day is worth more than five dollars."

A man who keeps his time will keep his word; in truth, he cannot keep his word unless he *does* keep his time.

When the Duchess of Sutherland came late, keeping the court waiting, the queen, who was always vexed by tardiness, presented her with her own watch, saying, "I am afraid your's does not keep good time."

"Then you must get a new watch, or I another secretary," replied Washington, when his secretary excused the lateness of his attendance by saying that his watch was too slow.

"I have generally found that a man who is good at an excuse is good for nothing else," said Franklin to a servant who was always late, but always ready with an excuse.

One of the best things about school and college life is that the bell which strikes the hour for rising, for recitations, or for lectures, teaches habits of promptness. Every young man should have a watch which is a good timekeeper; one that is *nearly* right encourages bad habits, and is an expensive investment at any price. Wear threadbare clothes if you must, but never carry an inaccurate watch.

"Five minutes behind time" has ruined many a man and many a firm.

"He who rises late," says Fuller, "must trot all day, and shall scarcely overtake his business at night."

Some people are too late for everything but ruin; when a nobleman apologized to George III. for being late, and said, "better late than never," the king replied, "No, I say, *better never than late.*"

"Better late than never" is not half so good a maxim as "Better never late."

If Samuel Budgett was even a minute late at an appointment he would apologize; he was as punctual as a chronometer. Punctuality is contagious.

Napoleon infused promptness into his officers every minute. What power there is in promptness to take the drudgery out of a disagreeable task.

"A singular mischance has happened to some of our friends," said Hamilton. "At the instant when He ushered them into existence, God gave them work to do, and He also gave them a competency of time; so much that if they began at the right moment and wrought with sufficient vigor, their time and their work would end together. But a good many years ago a strange misfortune befell them. A fragment of their allotted time was lost. They cannot tell what became of it, but sure enough, it has dropped out of existence; for just like two measuring lines laid alongside the one an inch shorter than the other, their work and their time run parallel, but the work is always ten minutes in advance of the time. They are not irregular. They are never too soon. Their letters are posted the very minute after the mail is closed. They arrive at the wharf just in time to see the steamboat off, they come in sight of the terminus precisely as the station gates are closing. They do not break any engagement nor neglect any duty; but they systematically go about it too late, and usually too late by about the same fatal interval."

Of Tours, the wealthy New Orleans ship-owner, it is said that he was as methodical and regular as a clock, and that his neighbors were in the habit of judging of the time of the day by his movements.

"How," asked a man of Sir Walter Raleigh, "do you accomplish so much and in so short a time?" "When I have anything do, I go and do it," was the reply. The man who always acts promptly, even if he makes occasional mistakes, will succeed when a procrastinator will fail—even if he have the better judgment.

When asked how he got through so much work, Lord Chesterfield replied: "Because I never put off till morrow what I can do to-day."

Dewitt, pensionary of Holland, answered the same question: "Nothing is more easy; never do but one thing at a time, and never put off until to-morrow what can be done to-day."

Walter Scott was a very punctual man. This was the secret of his enormous achievements. He made it a rule to answer all letters the day they were received. He rose at five. By breakfast time he had broken the neck of the day's work, as he used to say. Writing to a youth who had obtained a situation and asked him for advice, he gave this counsel: "Beware of stumbling over a propensity which easily besets you from not having your time fully employed—I mean what the women call dawdling. Do instantly whatever is to be done, and take the hours of recreation after business, never before it."

Frederick the Great had a maxim: "Time is the only treasure of which it is proper to be avaricious."

Leibnitz declared that "the loss of an hour is the loss of a part of life."

Napoleon, who knew the value of time, remarked that it was the quarter hours that won battles. The value of minutes has been often recognized, and any person watching a railway clerk handing out tickets and change during the last few minutes available must have been struck with how much could be done in these short periods of time.

At the appointed hour the train starts and by and by is carrying passengers at the rate of sixty miles an hour. In a second you are carried twenty-nine yards. In one twenty-ninth of a second you pass over one yard. Now, one yard is quite an appreciable distance, but one twenty-ninth of a second is a period which cannot be appreciated.

The father of the Webster brothers, before going away to be gone for a week, gave his boys a stint to cut a field of corn, telling them that after it was done, if they had any time left, they might do what they pleased. The boys looked the field over on Monday morning and concluded they could do all the work in three days, so they decided to play the first three days. Thursday morning they went to the field, but it looked so much larger than it did on Monday morning, that they decided they could not possibly do it in three days, and rather than not do it all, they would not touch it. When the angry father returned, he called Ezekiel to him and asked him why they had not harvested the corn. "What have you been doing?" said the stern father. "Nothing, father." "And what have you been doing, Daniel?" "Helping Zeke, sir."

How many boys, and men, too, waste hours and days "helping Zeke!"

"Remember the world was created in six days," said Napoleon to one of his officers. "Ask for whatever you please except time."

Railroads and steamboats have been wonderful educators in promptness. No matter who is late they leave right on the minute.

It is interesting to watch people at a great railroad station, running, hurrying, trying to make up time, for they well know when the time arrives the train will leave.

Factories, shops, stores, banks, everything opens and closes on the minute. The higher the state of civilization the prompter is everything done. In countries without railroads, as in Eastern countries, everything is behind time. Everybody is indolent and lazy.

The world knows that the prompt man's bills and notes will be paid on the day they are due, and will trust him. People will give him credit, for they know they can depend upon him. But lack of promptness will shake confidence almost as quickly as downright dishonesty. The man who has a habit of dawdling or listlessness will show it in everything he does. He is late at meals, late at work, dawdles on the street, loses his train, misses his appointments, and dawdles at his store until the banks are closed. Everybody he meets suffers more or less from his malady, for dawdling becomes practically a disease.

"You will never find time for anything," said Charles Buxton; "if you want time you must make it."

The best work we ever do is that which we do now, and can never repeat. "Too late," is the curse of the unsuccessful, who forget that "one to-day is worth two to-morrows."

Time accepts no sacrifice; it admits of neither redemption nor atonement. *It is the true avenger.* Your enemy may become your friend,—your injurer may do you justice,—but Time is inexorable, and has no mercy.

Then stay the present instant, dear Horatio:Imprint the marks of wisdom on its wings.'Tis of more worth than kingdoms! far more preciousThan all the crimson treasures of life's fountain.O! let it not elude thy grasp; but, likeThe good old patriarch upon record,Hold the fleet angel fast until he bless thee.—NATHANIEL COTTON.

CHAPTER XII

THOROUGHNESS

Doing well depends upon doing completely.—PERSIAN PROVERB.

He who does well will always have patrons enough.—PLAUTUS.

If a man can write a better book, preach a better sermon, or make a better mouse-trap than his neighbor, though he build his house in the woods, the world will make a beaten path to his door.—EMERSON.

I hate a thing done by halves. If it be right, do it boldly; if it be wrong, leave it undone.—GILPIN.

No two things differ more than Hurry and Dispatch. Hurry is the mark of a weak mind, Dispatch of a strong one. * * * Like a turnstile, he (the weak man) is in everybody's way, but stops nobody; he talks a great deal, but says very little; looks into everything, but sees nothing; and has a hundred irons in the fire, but very few of them are hot, and with those few that are he only burns his fingers.—COLTON.

"Make me as good a hammer as you know how," said a carpenter to the blacksmith in a New York village before the first railroad was built; "six of us have come to work on the new church, and I've left mine at home." "As good a one as I know how?" asked David Maydole, doubtfully, "but perhaps you don't want to pay for as good a one as I know how to make." "Yes, I do," said the carpenter, "I want a good hammer."

It was indeed a good hammer that he received, the best, probably, that had ever been made. By means of a longer hole than usual, David had wedged the handle in its place so that the head could not fly off, a wonderful improvement in the eyes of the carpenter, who boasted of his prize to his companions. They all came to the shop next day, and each ordered just such a hammer. When the contractor saw the tools, he ordered two for himself, asking that they be made a little better than those for his men. "I can't make any better ones," said Maydole; "when I make a thing, I make it as well as I can, no matter whom it is for."

The storekeeper soon ordered two dozen, a supply unheard of in his previous business career. A New York dealer in tools came to the village to sell his wares, and bought all the storekeeper had, and left a standing order for all the blacksmith could make. David might have grown very wealthy by making goods of the standard already attained; but throughout his long and successful life he never ceased to study still further to perfect his hammers in the minutest detail. They were usually sold without any warrant of excellence, the word "Maydole" stamped on the head being universally considered a guaranty of the best article the world could produce. Character is power, and is the best advertisement in the world.

"Yes," said he one day to the late James Parton, who told this story, "I have made hammers in this little village for twenty-eight years." "Well," replied the great historian, "by this time you ought to make a pretty good hammer."

"No, I can't," was the reply, "I can't make a pretty good hammer. I make the best hammer that's made. My only care is to make a perfect hammer. If folks don't want to pay me what they're worth, they're welcome to buy cheaper ones somewhere else. My wants are few, and I'm ready any time to go back to my blacksmith's shop, where I worked forty years ago, before I thought of making hammers. Then I had a boy to blow by bellows, now I have one hundred and fifteen men. Do you see them over there watching the heads cook over the charcoal furnace, as your cook, if she knows what she is about, watches the chops broiling? Each of them is hammered out of a piece of iron, and is tempered under the inspection of an experienced man. Every handle is seasoned three years, or until there is no shrink left in it. Once I thought I could use machinery in manufacturing them; now I know that a perfect tool can't be made by machinery, and every bit of the work is done by hand."

"In telling this little story," said Parton, "I have told thousands of stories. Take the word 'hammer' out of it, and put 'glue' in its place, and you have the history of Peter Cooper. By putting in other words, you can make the true history of every great business in the world which has lasted thirty years."

"We have no secret," said Manager Daniel J. Morrill, of the Cambria Iron Works, employing seven thousand men, at Johnstown, Pa. "We always try to beat our last batch of rails. That is all the secret we've got, and we don't care who knows it."

"I don't try to see how cheap a machine I can produce, but how good a machine," said the late John C. Whitin, of Northbridge, Mass., to a customer who complained of the high price of some cotton machinery. Business men soon learned what this meant; and when there was occasion to advertise any machinery for sale, New England cotton manufacturers were accustomed to state the number of years it had been in use and add, as an all-sufficient guaranty of Northbridge products, "Whitin make." Put thoroughness into your work: it pays.

"The accurate boy is always the favored one," said President Tuttle. If a carpenter must stand at his journeyman's elbow to be sure his work is right, or if a cashier must run over his bookkeeper's columns, he might as well do the work himself as employ another to do it in that way.

"Mr. Girard, can you not assist me by giving me a little work?" asked one John Smith, who had formerly worked for the great banker and attracted attention by his activity.

"Assistance—work—ah? You want work?" "Yes sir; it's a long time since I've had anything to do."

"Very well, I shall give you some. You see dem stone yondare?" "Yes, sir." "Very well; you shall fetch and put them in this place; you see?" "Yes sir." "And when you done, come to me at my bank."

Smith finished his task, reported to Mr. Girard, and asked for more work. "Ah, ha, oui. You want more work? Very well; you shall go place dem stone where you got him. Understandez? You take him back." "Yes, sir."

Again Smith performed the work and waited on Mr. Girard for payment. "Ah, ha, you all finish?" "Yes, sir." "Very well; how much money shall I give you?" "One dollar, sir." "Dat is honest. You take no advantage. Dare is your dollar." "Can I do anything else for you?" "Oui, come here when you get up to-morrow. You shall have more work."

Smith was punctual, but for the third time, and yet again for the fourth, he was ordered to "take dem stone back again." When he called for his pay in the evening Stephen Girard spoke very cordially. "Ah, Monsieur Smit, you shall be my man; you mind your own business and do it, ask no questions, you do not interfere. You got one vife?" "Yes, sir." "Ah, dat is bad. Von vife is bad. Any little chicks?" "Yes, sir, five living."

"Five? Dat is good; I like five. I like you, Monsieur Smit; you like to work; you mind your business. Now I do something for your five little chicks. There: take these five pieces of paper for your five little chicks; you shall work for them; you shall mind your own business, and your little chicks shall never want five more." In a few years Mr. Smith became one of the wealthiest and most respected merchants of Philadelphia.

It is difficult to estimate the great influence upon a life of the early formed habit of doing everything to a finish, not leaving it half done, or pretty nearly done, but completely done. Nature finishes every little leaf, even to every little rib, its edges and stem, as exactly and perfectly as though it were the only leaf to be made that year. Even the flower that blooms in the mountain dell, where no human eye will ever behold it, is finished with the same perfection and exactness of form and outline, with the same delicate shade of color, with the same completeness of beauty, as though it was made for royalty in the queen's garden. "Perfection to the finish" is a motto which every youth should adopt.

"How did you attain such excellence in your profession?" was asked of Sir Joshua Reynolds. "By observing one simple rule, namely, to make each picture the best," he replied.

The discipline of being exact is uplifting. Progress is never more rapid than it is when we are studying to be accurate. The effort educates all the powers. Arthur Helps says: "I do not know that there is anything except it be humility, which is so valuable, as an incident of education, as accuracy: and accuracy can be taught. Direct lies told to the world are as dust in the balance when weighed against the falsehoods of inaccuracy."

Too many youths enter upon their business in a languid, half-hearted way, and do their work in a slipshod manner. The consequence is that they inspire neither admiration nor confidence on the part of their superiors, and cut off almost every chance of success. There is a loose, perfunctory method of doing one's work that never merits advance, and very rarely wins it. Instead of buckling to their task with all the force they possess, they merely touch it with the tips of their fingers, their rule apparently being, the maximum of ease with the minimum of work. The principle of Strafford, the great minister of Charles I., is indicated by his motto, the one word "Thorough." It was said of King Hezekiah, "In every work that he began, he did it with all his heart and prospered."

The stone-cutter goes to work on a stone and most patiently shapes it. He carves that bit of fern, putting all his skill and taste into it. And by-and-by the master says, "Well done," and takes it away and gives him another block and tells him to work on that. And so he works on that from the rising of the sun till the going down of the same, and he only knows that he is earning his bread. And he continues to put all his skill and taste into his work. He has no idea what use will be made of these few stones which he has been carving, until afterward, when, one day, walking along the street, and looking up at the front of the Art Gallery, he sees the stones upon which he has worked. He did not know what they were for, but the architect did. And as he stands looking at his work on that structure which is the beauty of the whole street, he says: "I am glad I did it well." And every day as he passes that way, he says to himself exultingly, "I did it well." He did not draw the design, nor plan the building, and he knew nothing of what use was to be made of his work: but he took pains in cutting those stems; and when he saw they were a part of that magnificent structure, his soul rejoiced.

Work that is not finished, is not work at all; it is merely a botch. We often see this defect of incompleteness in a child, which increases in youth. All about the house, everywhere, there are half-finished things. It is true that children often become tired of things which they begin with enthusiasm; but there is a great difference in children about finishing what they undertake. A boy, for instance, will start out in the morning with great enthusiasm to dig his garden over; but, after a few minutes, his enthusiasm has evaporated, and he wants to go fishing. He soon becomes tired of this, and thinks he will make a boat. No sooner does he get a saw and knife and a few pieces of board about him than he makes up his mind that really what he wanted to do, after all, was to play ball, and this, in turn, must give way to something else.

One watch, set right, will do to set many by; but, on the other hand, one that goes wrong may be the means of misleading a whole neighborhood. The same may be said of the example we individually set to those around us.

"Whatever I have tried to do in life," said Dickens, "I have tried with all my heart to do well. What I have devoted myself to, I have devoted myself to completely."

It is no disgrace to be a shoemaker, but it is a disgrace for a shoemaker to make bad shoes.

A traveler, recently returned from Jerusalem, found, in conversation with Humboldt, that the latter was as conversant with the streets and houses of Jerusalem as he was himself. On being asked how long it was since he had visited it, the aged philosopher replied: "I have never been there; but I expected to go sixty years since, and I prepared myself."

So noted for excellency was everything bearing the brand of George Washington, that a barrel of flour marked "George Washington, Mount Vernon," was exempted from the customary inspection in the West India ports.

Pascal, the most wonderful mathematical genius of his time, whose work on conic sections, at sixteen, Descartes refused to believe could be produced at that age, is considered to have fixed the French language, as Luther did the German, by his writings. None of his provincial letters, with the exception of the last three, was more than eight quarto pages in length, yet he devoted twenty days to the writing of a single letter, and one of them was written no less than thirteen times.

The night the Tasmania was wrecked, the captain had given the course north by west, sixty-seven degrees. He had taken account of eddies and currents. The second officer, overlooking these, ordered the helmsman to make it north by west, fifty-seven degrees, but to bring the ship around so gently that the captain wouldn't know it. Hence her destruction.

Rev. Mr. Maley, of the Ohio Conference of the Methodist Church, had the habit of greatly exaggerating anything he talked about. His brethren at conference told him that this habit was growing on him, and rendering him unpopular in the ministry. Mr. Maley heard them patiently, and then said: "Brethren, I am aware of the truth of all you have said, and have shed barrels of tears over it."

There is a great difference between going just right and a little wrong.

CHAPTER XIII

TRIFLES

In the elder days of ArtBuilders wrought with greatest careEach minute and unseen part,For the gods see everywhere.—LONGFELLOW.

Think naught a trifle, though it small appear,Small sands the mountain, moments make the year,And trifles, life.—YOUNG.

The smallest hair throws its shadow.—GOETHE.

He that despiseth small things shall fall little by little.—ECCLESIASTES.

It is the little rift within the lute,That by and by will make the music mute,And ever widening slowly silence all.—TENNYSON.

"A pebble in the streamlet scantHas turned the course of many a river:A dewdrop on the baby plantHas warped the giant oak forever."

It is the close observation of little things which is the secret of success in business, in art, in science, and in every pursuit of life.—SMILES.

"Only!—But then the onlysMake up the mighty all."

"My rule of conduct has been that whatever is worth doing at all is worth doing well," said Nicolas Poussin, the great French painter. When asked the reason why he had become so eminent in a land of famous artists he replied, "Because I have neglected nothing."

"Do little things now," says a Persian proverb; "so shall big things come to thee by and by asking to be done." God will take care of the great things if we do not neglect the little ones.

A gentleman advertised for a boy to assist him in his office, and nearly fifty applicants presented themselves to him. Out of the whole number he in a short time selected one and dismissed the rest. "I should like to know," said a friend, "on what ground you selected that boy, who had not a single recommendation?" "You are mistaken," said the gentleman, "he had a great many. He wiped his feet when he came in, and closed the door after him, showing that he was careful. He gave up his seat instantly to that lame old man, showing that he was kind and thoughtful. He took off his cap when he came in, and answered my questions promptly and respectfully, showing that he was polite and gentlemanly. He picked up the book which I had purposely laid upon the floor, and replaced it on the table, while all the rest stepped over it, or shoved it aside; and he waited quietly for his turn, instead of pushing and crowding, showing that he was honest and orderly. When I talked to him, I noticed that his clothes were carefully brushed, his hair in nice order, and his teeth as white as milk; and when he wrote his name, I noticed that his finger-nails were clean, instead of being tipped with jet, like that handsome little fellow's, in the blue jacket. Don't you call those letters of recommendation? I do; and I would give more for what I can tell about a boy by using my eyes ten minutes, than for all the fine letters he can bring me."

"Least of all seeds, greatest of all harvests," seems to be one of the great laws of nature. All life comes from microscopic beginnings. In nature there is nothing small. The microscope reveals as great a world below as the telescope above. All of nature's laws govern the smallest atoms, and a single drop of water is a miniature ocean.

"I cannot see that you have made any progress since my last visit," said a gentleman to Michael Angelo. "But," said the sculptor, "I have retouched this part, polished that, softened that feature, brought out that muscle, given some expression to this lip, more energy to that limb, etc." "But they are trifles!" exclaimed the visitor. "It may be so," replied the great artist, "but trifles make perfection, and perfection is no trifle." That infinite patience which made Michael Angelo spend a week in bringing out a muscle in a statue with more vital fidelity to truth, or Gerhard Dow a day in giving the right effect to a dewdrop on a cabbage leaf, makes all the difference between success and failure.

"Of what use is it?" people asked with a sneer, when Franklin told of his discovery that lightning and electricity are identical. "What is the use of a child?" replied Franklin; "it may become a man."

In the earliest days of cotton spinning, the small fibres would stick to the bobbins, and make it necessary to stop and clear the machinery. Although this loss of time reduced the earnings of the operatives, the father of Robert Peel noticed that one of his spinners always drew full pay, as his machine never stopped. "How is this, Dick?" asked Mr. Peel one day; "the on-looker tells me your bobbins are always clean." "Ay, that they be," replied Dick Ferguson. "How do you manage it, Dick?" "Why, you see, Meester Peel," said the workman, "it is sort o' secret! If I tow'd ye, yo'd be as wise as I am." "That's so," said Mr. Peel, smiling; "but I'd give you something to know. Could you make all the looms work as smoothly as yours?" "Ivery one of 'em, meester," replied Dick. "Well, what shall I give you for your secret?" asked Mr. Peel, and Dick replied, "Gi' me a quart of ale every day as I'm in the mills, and I'll tell thee all about it." "Agreed," said Mr. Peel, and Dick whispered very cautiously in his ear, "Chalk your bobbins!" That was the whole secret, and Mr. Peel soon shot ahead of all his competitors, for he made machines that would chalk their own bobbins. Dick was handsomely rewarded with money instead of beer. His little idea has saved the world millions of dollars.

The totality of a life at any moment is the product mainly of little things. Trifling choices, insignificant exercises of the will, unimportant acts often repeated,—things seemingly of small account,—these are the thousand tiny sculptors that are carving away constantly at the rude block of our life, giving it shape and feature. Indeed the formation of character is much like the work of an artist in stone. The sculptor takes a rough, unshapen mass of marble, and with strong, rapid strokes of mallet and chisel quickly brings into view the rude outline of his design; but after the outline appears then come hours, days, perhaps even years, of patient, minute labor. A novice might see no change in the statue from one day to another; for though the chisel touches the stone a thousand times, it touches as lightly as the fall of a rain-drop, but each touch leaves a mark.

The smallest thing becomes respectable when regarded as the commencement of what has advanced or is advancing into magnificence. The crude settlement of Romulus would have remained an insignificant circumstance and might have justly sunk into oblivion, if Rome had not at length commanded the world.

Beecher says that men, in their property, are afraid of conflagrations and lightning strokes; but if they were building a wharf in Panama, a million madrepores, so small that only the microscope could detect them, would begin to bore the piles down under the water. There would be neither noise nor foam; but in a little while, if a child did but touch the post, over it would fall as if a saw had cut it through.

Men think, with regard to their conduct, that, if they were to lift themselves up gigantically and commit some crashing sin, they should never be able to hold up their heads; but they will harbor in their souls little sins, which are piercing and eating them away to inevitable ruin.

Lichens, of themselves of little value, prepare the way for important vegetation. They deposit, in dying, an acid which wears away the rock and prepares the mould necessary for the nourishment of superior plants.

It was but a tiny rivulet trickling down the embankment that started the terrible Johnstown flood and swept thousands into eternity. One noble heroic act has elevated a nation. Franklin's whole career was changed by a torn copy of Cotton Mather's Essays to Do Good. Taking up a stone to throw at a turtle was the turning point in Theodore Parker's life. As he raised the stone something within him said, "Don't do it," and he didn't. He went home and asked his mother what it was in him that said "don't." She told him it was conscience. Small things become great when a great soul sees them. A child, when asked why a certain tree grew crooked, answered, "Somebody trod upon it when it was a little fellow."

By gnawing through a dike, even a rat may drown a nation. A little boy in Holland saw water trickling from a small hole near the bottom of a dike. He realized that the leak would rapidly become larger if the water was not checked, so he held his hand over the hole for hours on a dark and dismal night until he could attract the attention of passers-by. His name is still held in grateful remembrance in Holland.

We may tell which way the wind blew before the Deluge by marking the ripple and cupping of the rain in the petrified sand now preserved forever. We tell the very path by which gigantic creatures, whom man never saw, walked to the river's edge to find their food.

The tears of Virgilia and Volumnia saved Rome from the Volscians when nothing else could move the vengeful heart of Coriolanus.

 Not even Helen of Troy, it is said, was beautiful enough to spare the tip of her nose; and if Cleopatra's had been an inch shorter Mark Antony would never have become infatuated with her wonderful charms, and the blemish would have changed the history of the world. Anne Boleyn's fascinating smile split the great Church of Rome in twain, and gave a nation an altered destiny. Napoleon, who feared not to attack the proudest monarchs in their capitals, shrank from the political influence of one independent woman in private life, Madame de Staël.

It was a little thing for a cow to kick over a lantern left in a shanty, but it laid Chicago in ashes, and rendered homeless a hundred thousand people.

The discovery of glass was due to a mere accident—the building of a fire on the sand; and the bayonet, first made at Bayonne, in France, owes its existence to the fact that a Basque regiment, being hard pressed by the enemy, one of the soldiers suggested that, as their ammunition was exhausted, they should fix their long knives into the barrels of their muskets, which was done, and the first bayonet-charge was made.

A jest led to a war between two great nations. The presence of a comma in a deed, lost to the owner of an estate five thousand dollars a month for eight months. The battle of Corunna was fought and Sir John Moore's life sacrificed, in 1809, through a dragoon stopping to drink while bearing despatches.

"You do no work," said the scissors to the rivet. "Where would your work be," said the rivet to the scissors, "if I didn't keep you together?"

Every day is a little life; and our whole life but a day repeated. Those that dare lose a day are dangerously prodigal; those that dare misspend it, desperate. What is the happiness of your life made up of? Little courtesies, little kindnesses, pleasant words, genial smiles, a friendly letter, good wishes, and good deeds. One in a million—once in a lifetime—may do a heroic action.

We call the large majority of human lives *obscure*. Presumptuous that we are! How know we what lives a single thought retained from the dust of nameless graves may have lighted to renown?

CHAPTER XIV

COURAGE

Quit yourselves like men.—1 Samuel iv. 9

Cowards have no luck.—Elizabeth Kulman.

He has not learned the lesson of life who does not every day surmount a fear.—Emerson.

To dare is better than to doubt,For doubt is always grieving;'Tis faith that finds the riddles out;The prize is for believing.—Henry Burton.

—WalkBoldly and wisely in that light thou hast;There is a hand above will help thee on.—Bailey's Festus.

"Have hope! Though clouds environ now,And gladness hides her face in scorn,Put thou the shadow from thy brow—No night but hath its morn."

"Our enemies are before us," exclaimed the Spartans at Thermopylæ. "And we are before them," was the cool reply of Leonidas. "Deliver your arms," came the message from Xerxes. "Come and take them," was the answer Leonidas sent back. A Persian soldier said: "You will not be able to see the sun for flying javelins and arrows." "Then we will fight in the shade," replied a Lacedemonian. What wonder that a handful of such men checked the march of the greatest host that ever trod the earth.

"The hero," says Emerson, "is the man who is immovably centred."

Darius the Great sent ambassadors to the Athenians, to demand earth and water, which denoted submission. The Athenians threw them into a ditch and told them, there was earth and water enough.

"Bring back the colors," shouted a captain at the battle of the Alma, when an ensign maintained his ground in front, although the men were retreating. "No," cried the ensign, "bring up the men to the colors." "To dare, and again to dare, and without end to dare," was Danton's noble defiance to the enemies of France.

Shakespeare says: "He is not worthy of the honeycomb that shuns the hives because the bees have stings."

"It is a bad omen," said Eric the Red, when his horse slipped and fell on the way to his ship, moored on the coast of Greenland, in readiness for a voyage of discovery. "Ill-fortune would be mine should I dare venture now upon the sea." So he returned to his house; but his young son Leif decided to go, and with a crew of thirty-five men, sailed southward in search of the unknown shore upon which Captain Biarni had been driven by a storm, while sailing in another Viking ship two or three years before. The first land that they saw was probably Labrador, a barren, rugged plain. Leif called this country Heluland, or the land of flat stones. Sailing onward many days, he came to a low, level coast thickly covered with woods, on account of which he called the country Markland, probably the modern Nova Scotia. Sailing onward, they came to an island which they named Vinland, on account of the abundance of delicious wild grapes in the woods. This was in the year 1000. Here where the city of Newport, R. I., stands, they spent many months, and then returned to Greenland with their vessel loaded with grapes and strange kinds of wood. The voyage was successful, and no doubt Eric was sorry he had been frightened by the bad omen.

"Not every vessel that sails from Tarshish will bring back the Gold of Ophir. But shall it therefore rot in the harbor? No! Give its sails to the wind!"

Men who have dared have moved the world, often before reaching the prime of life. It is astonishing what daring to begin and perseverance have enabled even youths to achieve. Alexander, who ascended the throne at twenty, had conquered the whole known world before dying at thirty-three. Julius Cæsar captured eight hundred cities, conquered three hundred nations, and defeated three million men, became a great orator and one of the greatest statesmen known, and still was a young man. Washington was appointed adjutant-general at nineteen, was sent at twenty-one as an ambassador to treat with the French, and won his first battle as a colonel at twenty-two. Lafayette was made general of the whole French army at twenty. Charlemagne was master of France and Germany at thirty. Condé was only twenty-two when he conquered at Rocroi. Galileo was but eighteen when he saw the principle of the pendulum in the swinging lamp in the cathedral at Pisa. Peel was in Parliament at twenty-one. Gladstone was in Parliament before he was twenty-two, and at twenty-four he was a Lord of the Treasury. Elizabeth Barrett Browning was proficient in Greek and Latin at twelve; De Quincey at eleven. Robert Browning wrote at eleven poetry of no mean order. Cowley, who sleeps in Westminster Abbey, published a volume of poems at fifteen. N. P. Willis won lasting fame as a poet before leaving college. Macaulay was a celebrated author before he was twenty-three. Luther was but twenty-nine when he nailed his famous thesis to the door of the bishop and defied the pope. Nelson was a lieutenant in the British navy before he was twenty. He was but forty-seven when he received his death wound at Trafalgar. Charles the Twelfth was only nineteen when he gained the battle of Narva; at thirty-six Cortes was the conqueror of Mexico; at thirty-two Clive had established the British power in India. Hannibal, the greatest of military commanders, was only thirty when, at Cannæ, he dealt an almost annihilating blow at the Republic of Rome; and Napoleon was only twenty-seven when, on the plains of Italy, he out-generaled and defeated, one after another, the veteran marshals of Austria.

Equal courage and resolution are often shown by men who have passed the allotted limit of life. Victor Hugo and Wellington were both in their prime after they had reached the age of threescore years and ten. George Bancroft wrote some of his best historical work when he was eighty-five. Gladstone ruled England with a strong hand at eighty-four, and was a marvel of literary and scholarly ability.

"Your Grace has not the organ of animal courage largely developed," said a phrenologist, who was examining Wellington's head. "You are right," replied the Iron Duke, "and but for my sense of duty I should have retreated in my first fight." That first fight, on an Indian field, was one of the most terrible on record.

Grant never knew when he was beaten. When told that he was surrounded by the enemy at Belmont, he quietly replied: "Well, then, we must cut our way out."

When General Jackson was a judge and was holding court in a small settlement, a border ruffian, a murderer and desperado, came into the court-room with brutal violence and interrupted the court. The judge ordered him to be arrested. The officer did not dare approach him. "Call a posse," said the judge, "and arrest him." But they also shrank with fear from the ruffian. "Call me, then," said Jackson; "this court is adjourned for five minutes." He left the bench, walked straight up to the man, and with his eagle eye actually cowed the ruffian, who dropped his weapons, afterward saying: "There was something in his eye I could not resist."

Lincoln never shrank from espousing an unpopular cause when he believed it to be right. At the time when it almost cost a young lawyer his bread and butter to defend the fugitive slave, and when other lawyers had refused, Lincoln would always plead the cause of the unfortunate whenever an opportunity presented. "Go to Lincoln," people would say, when these bounded fugitives were seeking protection; "he's not afraid of any cause, if it's right."

Abraham Lincoln's boyhood was one long struggle with poverty, with little education and no influential friends. When at last he had begun the practice of law it required no little daring to cast his fortune with the weaker side in politics, and thus imperil what small reputation he had gained. Only the most sublime moral courage could have sustained him as President to hold his ground against hostile criticism and a long train of disaster; to issue the Emancipation Proclamation; to support Grant and Stanton against the clamor of the politicians and the press; and through it all to do the right as God gave him to see the right.

"Doubt indulged becomes doubt realized." To determine to do anything is half the battle. "To think a thing is impossible is to make it so." "Courage is victory, timidity is defeat."

Don't waste time dreaming of obstacles you may never encounter, or in crossing bridges you have not reached. Don't fool with a nettle! Grasp with firmness if you would rob it of its sting. To half will and to hang forever in the balance is to lose your grip on life.

Execute your resolutions immediately. Thoughts are but dreams till their effects be tried. Does competition trouble you? work away; what is your competitor but a man? *Conquer your place in the world*, for all things serve a brave soul. Combat difficulty manfully; sustain misfortune bravely; endure poverty nobly; encounter disappointment courageously. The influence of the brave man is a magnetism which creates an epidemic of noble zeal in all about him. Every day sends to the grave obscure men, who have only remained in obscurity because their timidity has prevented them from making a first effort; and who, if they could have been induced to begin, would in all probability have gone great lengths in the career of usefulness and fame. "No great deed is done," says George Eliot, "by falterers who ask for certainty."

A mouse that dwelt near the abode of a great magician was kept in such constant distress by its fear of a cat that the magician, taking pity on it, turned it into a cat itself. Immediately it began to suffer from its fear of a dog, so the magician turned it into a dog. Then it began to suffer from fear of a tiger, and the magician turned it into a tiger. Then it began to suffer from its fear of huntsmen, and the magician, in disgust, said, "Be a mouse again. As you have only the heart of a mouse it is impossible to help you by giving you the body of a nobler animal." And the poor creature again became a mouse.

Young Commodore Oliver H. Perry, not twenty-eight years old, was intrusted with the plan to gain control of Lake Erie. With great energy Perry directed the construction of nine ships, carrying fifty-four guns, and conquered Commodore Barclay, a veteran of European navies, with six vessels, carrying sixty-three guns. Perry had no experience in naval battles before this.

To believe a business impossible is the way to make it so. Feasible projects often miscarry through despondency, and are strangled at birth by a cowardly imagination. A ship on a lee shore stands out to sea to escape shipwreck. Shrink and you will be despised.

One of Napoleon's drummer boys won the battle of Arcola. Napoleon's little army of fourteen thousand men had fought fifty thousand Austrians for seventy-two hours; the Austrians' position enabled them to sweep the bridge of Arcola, which the French had gained and which they must hold to win the battle. The drummer boy, on the shoulders of his sergeant (who swam across the river with him), beat the drum all the way across the river, and when on the opposite end of the bridge he beat his drum so vigorously that the Austrians, remembering the terrible French onslaught of the day before, fled in terror, thinking the French army was advancing upon them. Napoleon dated his great confidence in himself from this drum. This boy's heroic act was represented in stone on the front of the Pantheon of Paris.

Two days before the battle of Jena Napoleon said: "My lads, you must not fear death: when soldiers brave death they drive him into the enemy's ranks."

Arago says, in his autobiography, that when he was puzzled and discouraged with difficulties he met with in his early studies in mathematics some words he found on the waste leaf of his text-book caught his attention and interested him. He found it to be a short letter from D'Alembert to a young person, disheartened like himself, and read: "Go on, sir, go on. The difficulties you meet with will resolve themselves as you advance. Proceed and light will dawn and shine with increasing clearness on your path." "That maxim," he said, "was my greatest master in mathematics."

Overtaken near a rocky coast by a sudden storm of great violence, the captain of a French brig gave orders to put out to sea; but in spite of all the efforts of the crew they could not steer clear of the rocks, and after struggling for a whole day they felt a violent shock, accompanied by a horrible crash. The boats were lowered, but only to be swept away by the waves. As a last resort the captain proposed that some sailors should swim ashore with a rope, but not a man would volunteer.

"Captain," said the little twelve-year-old cabin boy, Jacques, timidly, "You don't wish to expose the lives of good sailors like these; it does not matter what becomes of a little cabin boy. Give me a ball of strong string, which will unroll as I go on; fasten one end around my body, and I promise you that within an hour the rope shall be well fastened to the shore or I will perish in the attempt."

Before anyone could stop him he leaped overboard. His head was soon seen like a black point rising above the waves and then it disappeared in the distance and mist, and but for the occasional pull upon the ball of cord all would have thought him dead. At length it fell as if slackened and the sailors looked at one another in silence, when a quick, violent pull, followed by a second and a third, told that Jacques had reached the shore. A strong rope was fastened to the cord and pulled to the shore, and by its aid many of the sailors were rescued.

In 1833 Miss Prudence Crandall, a Quaker schoolmistress of Canterbury, Conn., opened her school to negro children as well as to whites. The whole place was thrown into uproar; town meetings were called to denounce her; the most vindictive and inhuman measures were taken to isolate the school from the support of the townspeople; stores and churches were closed against teacher and pupils; public conveyances were denied them; physicians would not attend them; Miss Crandall's own friends dared not visit her; the house was assailed with rotten eggs and stones and finally set on fire. Yet the cause was righteous and the opposition proved vain and fruitless. Public opinion is often radically wrong.

Staunch old Admiral Farragut—he of the true heart and the iron will—said to another officer of the navy, "Dupont, do you know why you didn't get into Charleston with your ironclads?" "Oh, it was because the channel was so crooked." "No, Dupont, it was not that." "Well, the rebel fire was perfectly horrible." "Yes, but it wasn't that." "What was it, then?" "*It was because you didn't believe you could go in.*"

"I have tried Lord Howe on most important occasions. He never asked me *how* he was to execute any service entrusted to his charge, but always went straight forward and *did it.*" So answered Sir Edward Hawke, when his appointment of Howe for some peculiarly responsible duty was criticized on the ground that Howe was the junior admiral in the fleet.

There is a tradition among the Indians that Manitou was traveling in the invisible world and came upon a hedge of thorns, then saw wild beasts glare upon him from the thicket, and after awhile stood before an impassable river. As he determined to proceed, the thorns turned out phantoms, the wild beasts powerless ghosts, and the river only a shadow. When we march on obstacles disappear. Many distinguished foreign and American statesmen were present at a fashionable dinner party where wine was freely poured, but Schuyler Colfax, then Vice-President of the United States, declined to drink from a proffered cup. "Colfax does not drink," sneered a Senator who had already taken too much. "You are right," said the Vice-President, "I dare not."

A Western party recently invited the surviving Union and Confederate officers to give an account of the bravest act observed by each during the Civil War. Colonel Thomas W. Higginson said that at a dinner at Beaufort, S. C., where wine flowed freely and ribald jests were bandied, Dr. Miner, a slight, boyish fellow who did not drink, was told that he could not go until he had drunk a toast, told a story, or sung a song. He replied: "I cannot sing, but I will give a toast, although I must drink it in water. It is 'Our Mothers.'" The men were so affected and ashamed that some took him by the hand and thanked him for displaying courage greater than that required to walk up to the mouth of a cannon.

When Grant was in Houston several years ago, he was given a rousing reception. Naturally hospitable, and naturally inclined to like a man of Grant's make-up, the Houstonites determined to go beyond any other Southern city in the way of a banquet and other manifestations of their good-will and hospitality. They made great preparations for the dinner, the committee taking great pains to have the finest wines that could be procured for the table at night. When the time came to serve the wine, the head-waiter went first to Grant. Without a word the general quietly turned down all the glasses at his plate. This movement was a great surprise to the Texans, but they were equal to the occasion. Without a single word being spoken, every man along the line of the long tables turned his glasses down, and there was not a drop of wine taken that night.

Don't be like Uriah Heep, begging everybody's pardon for taking the liberty of being in the world. There is nothing attractive in timidity, nothing lovable in fear. Both are deformities and are repulsive. Manly courage is dignified and graceful. The worst manners in the world are those of persons conscious "of being beneath their position, and trying to conceal it or make up for it by style." It takes courage for a young man to stand firmly erect while others are bowing and fawning for praise and power. It takes courage to wear threadbare clothes while your comrades dress in broadcloth. It takes courage to remain in honest poverty when others grow rich by fraud. It takes courage to say "No" squarely when those around you say "Yes." It takes courage to do your duty in silence and obscurity while others prosper and grow famous although neglecting sacred obligations. It takes courage to unmask your true self, to show your blemishes to a condemning world, and to pass for what you really are.

CHAPTER XV

WILL-POWER

In the moral world there is nothing impossible if we can bring a thorough will to do it.—W. HUMBOLDT.

It is firmness that makes the gods on our side.—VOLTAIRE.

Stand firm, don't flutter.—FRANKLIN.

People do not lack strength they lack will.—VICTOR HUGO.

Perpetual pushing and assurance put a difficulty out of countenance and make a seeming difficulty give way.—JEREMY COLLIER.

When a firm, decisive spirit is recognized, it is curious to see how the space clears around a man and leaves him room and freedom.—JOHN FOSTER.

"Do you know," asked Balzac's father, "that in literature a man must be either a king or a beggar?" "Very well," replied his son, "*I will be a king.*" After ten years of struggle with hardship and poverty, he won success as an author.

"Why do you repair that magistrate's bench with such great care?" asked a bystander of a carpenter who was taking unusual pains. "Because I wish to make it easy against the time when I come to sit on it myself," replied the other. He did sit on that bench as a magistrate a few years later.

"*I will be marshal of France and a great general,*" exclaimed a young French officer as he paced his room with hands tightly clenched. He became a successful general and a marshal of France.

"There is so much power in faith," says Bulwer, "even when faith is applied but to things human and earthly, that let a man but be firmly persuaded that he is born to do some day, what at the moment seems impossible, and it is fifty to one but what he does it before he dies."

There is about as much chance of idleness and incapacity winning real success, or a high position in life, as there would be in producing a Paradise Lost by shaking up promiscuously the separate words of Webster's Dictionary, and letting them fall at random on the floor. Fortune smiles upon those who roll up their sleeves and put their shoulders to the wheel; upon men who are not afraid of dreary, dry, irksome drudgery, men of nerve and grit who do not turn aside for dirt and detail.

"Is there one whom difficulties dishearten?" asked John Hunter. "He will do little. Is there one who will conquer? That kind of a man never fails."

"Circumstances," says Milton, "have rarely favored famous men. They have fought their way to triumph through all sorts of opposing obstacles."

"We have a half belief," said Emerson, "that the person is possible who can counterpoise all other persons. We believe that there may be a man *who is a match for events*,—one who never found his match,—against whom other men being dashed are broken,—one who can give you any odds and beat you."

The simple truth is that a will strong enough to keep a man continually striving for things not wholly beyond his powers will carry him in time very far toward his chosen goal.

At nineteen Bayard Taylor walked to Philadelphia, thirty miles, to find a publisher for fifteen of his poems. He wanted to see them printed in a book; but no publisher would undertake it. He returned to his home whistling, however, showing that his courage and resolution had not abated.

In Europe he was often forced to live on twenty cents a day for weeks on account of his poverty. He returned to London with only thirty cents left. He tried to sell a poem of twelve hundred lines, which he had in his knapsack, but no publisher wanted it. Of that time he wrote: "My situation was about as hopeless as it is possible to conceive." But his will defied circumstances and he rose above them. For two years he lived on two hundred and fifty dollars a year in London, earning every dollar of it with his pen.

His untimely death in 1879, at fifty-four, when Minister to Berlin, was lamented by the learned and great of all countries.

We are told of a young New York inventor who about twenty years ago spent every dollar he was worth in an experiment, which, if successful, would introduce his invention to public notice and insure his fortune, and, what he valued more, his usefulness. The next morning the daily papers heaped unsparing ridicule upon him. Hope for the future seemed vain. He looked around the shabby room where his wife, a delicate little woman, was preparing breakfast. He was without a penny. He seemed like a fool in his own eyes; all these years of hard work were wasted. He went into his chamber, sat down, and buried his face in his hands.

At length, with a fiery heat flashing through his body, he stood erect. "It *shall* succeed!" he said, shutting his teeth. His wife was crying over the papers when he went back. "They are very cruel," she said. "They don't understand." "I'll make them understand," he replied cheerfully. "It was a fight for six years," he said afterward. "Poverty, sickness and contempt followed me. I had nothing left but the *dogged determination* that it should succeed." It did succeed. The invention was a great and useful one. The inventor is now a prosperous and happy man.

Napoleon was a terrible example of what the power of will can accomplish. He always threw his whole force of body and mind direct upon his work. Imbecile rulers and the nations they governed went down before him in succession. He was told that the Alps stood in the way of his armies,—"There shall be no Alps," he said, and the road across the Simplon was constructed, through a district formerly almost inaccessible. "Impossible," said he, "is a word only to be found in the dictionary of fools." He was a man who toiled terribly; sometimes employing and exhausting four secretaries at a time. He spared no one, not even himself. His influence inspired other men, and put a new life into them. "I made my generals out of mud," he said.

To think we are able is almost to be so—to determine upon attainment, is frequently attainment itself. Thus, earnest resolution has often seemed to have about it almost a savor of omnipotence. The strength of Suwarrow's character lay in his power of willing, and, like most resolute persons, he preached it up as a system.

Before Pizarro, D'Almagro and De Luque obtained any associates or arms or soldiers, and with a very imperfect knowledge of the country or the powers they were to encounter, they celebrated a solemn mass in one of the great churches, dedicating themselves to the conquest of Peru. The people expressed their contempt at such a monstrous project, and were shocked at such sacrilege. But these decided men continued the service and afterward retired for their great preparation with an entire insensibility to the expressions of contempt. Their firmness was absolutely invincible. The world has deplored the results of this expedition, but there is a great lesson for us in the firmness of decision of its leaders. Such firmness would keep to its course and retain its purpose unshaken amidst the ruins of the world.

At the battle of Marengo the French army was supposed to be defeated; but, while Bonaparte and his staff were considering their next move, Dessaix suggested that there was yet time to retrieve their disaster, as it was only about the middle of the afternoon. Napoleon rallied his men, renewed the fight, and won a great victory over the Austrians, though the unfortunate Dessaix lost his own life on that field.

What has chance ever done in the world? Has it built any cities? Has it invented any telephones, any telegraphs? Has it built any steamships, established any universities, any asylums, any hospitals? Was there any chance in Cæsar's crossing the Rubicon? What had chance to do with Napoleon's career, with Wellington's, or Grant's, or Von Moltke's? Every battle was won before it was begun. What had luck to do with Thermopylæ, Trafalgar, Gettysburg? Our successes we ascribe to ourselves; our failures to destiny.

A vacillating man, no matter what his abilities, is invariably pushed to the wall in the race of life by a determined will. It is he who resolves to succeed, and who at every fresh rebuff begins resolutely again, that reaches the goal. The shores of fortune are covered with the stranded wrecks of men of brilliant ability, but who have wanted courage, faith and decision, and have therefore perished in sight of more resolute but less capable adventurers, who succeeded in making port. Hundreds of men go to their graves in obscurity, who have been obscure only because they lacked the pluck to make a first effort, and who, could they only have resolved to begin, would have astonished the world by their achievements and successes. The fact is, as Sydney Smith has well said, that in order to do anything in this world that is worth doing, we must not stand shivering on the bank, and thinking of the cold and the danger, but jump in and scramble through as well as we can.

Is not this a grand privilege of man, immortal man, that though he may not be able to stir a finger; that though a moth may crush him; that merely by a righteous will, he is raised above the stars; that by it he originates a good in the universe, which the universe could not annihilate; a good which can defy extinction, though all created energies of intelligence or matter were combined against it?

A man whose moral nature is ascendant is not the subject, but the superior of circumstances. He is free; nay, more, he is a king; and though this sovereignty may have been won by many desperate battles, once on the throne, and holding the sceptre with a firm grasp, he has a royalty of which neither time nor accident can strip him.

What can you do with a man who has an invincible purpose in him; who never knows when he is beaten; and who, when his legs are shot off, will fight on the stumps? Difficulties and opposition do not daunt him. He thrives upon persecution; it only stimulates him to more determined endeavor. Give a man the alphabet and an iron will, and who shall place bounds to his achievements! Imprison a Galileo for his discoveries in science, and he will experiment with the straw in his cell. Deprive Euler of his eyesight, and he but studies harder upon mental problems, thus developing marvelous powers of mathematical calculation. Lock up the poor Bedford tinker in jail, and he will write the finest allegory in the world, or will leave his imperishable thoughts upon the walls of his cell. Burn the body of Wycliffe and throw the ashes into the Severn; but they will be swept to the ocean, which will carry them, permeated with his principles, to all lands. *The world always listens to a man with a will in him.* You might as well snub the sun as such men as Bismarck and Grant.

Hope would storm the castle of despair; it gives courage when despondency would give up the battle of life. He is the best doctor who can implant *hope* and courage in the human soul. So he is the greatest man who can inspire us to the grandest achievements.

"Our remedies oft in ourselves do lie,Which we ascribe to heaven; the fated skyGives us free scope; and only backward pullsOur slow designs when we ourselves are dull."

"How much I could do if I only tried."

CHAPTER XVI

GUARD YOUR WEAK POINT

He that is slow to anger is better than the mighty: and he that ruleth his spirit than he that taketh a city.—BIBLE.

The first and best of victories is for a man to conquer himself: to be conquered by himself is, of all things, the most shameful and vile.—PLATO.

The worst education which teaches self-denial is better than the best which teaches everything else and not that.—JOHN STERLING.

Most powerful is he who has himself in his own power.—SENECA.

The energy which issues in growth, or assimilates knowledge, must originate in self and be self-directed.—THOMAS J. MORGAN.

The foes with which they waged their strifeWere passion, self and sin;The victories that laureled life,Were fought and won within.—EDWARD H. DEWART.

"I'll sign it after awhile," a drunkard would reply, when repeatedly urged by his wife to sign the pledge; "but I don't like to break off at once, the best way is to get used to a thing." "Very well, old man," said his wife, "see if you don't fall into a hole one of these days, with no one to help you out."

Not long after, when intoxicated, he did fall into a shallow well, but his shouts for help were fortunately heard by his wife. "Didn't I tell you so?" she asked. "It's lucky I was in hearing or you might have drowned." He took hold of the bucket and she tugged at the windlass; but when he was near the top her grasp slipped and down he went into the water again. This was repeated until he screamed: "Look here, you're doing that on purpose, I know you are." "Well, now, I am," admitted the wife. "Don't you remember telling me it's best to get used to a thing by degrees? I'm afraid if I bring you up sudden, you would not find it wholesome." Finding that his case was becoming desperate, he promised to sign the pledge at once. His wife raised him out immediately, but warned him that if ever he became intoxicated and fell into the well again, she would leave him there.

A man captured a young tiger and resolved to make a pet of it. It grew up like a kitten, fond and gentle. There was no evidence of its savage, bloodthirsty nature, and it seemed perfectly harmless. But one day while the master was playing with his pet, the rough tongue upon his hand started the blood from a scratch. The moment the beast tasted blood, his ferocious tiger nature was roused, and he rushed upon his master to tear him to pieces. Sometimes the appetite for drink, which was thought to be buried years ago, is roused by the taste or the smell of "the devil in solution," and the wretched victim finds himself a helpless slave to the passion which he thought dead.

When a young man, Hugh Miller once drank the two glasses of whiskey which fell to his share at the usual treat of drink of the masons with whom he worked. On reaching home he tried to read Bacon's Essays, his favorite book, but he could not distinguish the letters or comprehend the meaning. "The condition into which I had brought myself was, I felt, one of degradation," said he. "I had sunk, by my own act, for the time, to a lower level of intelligence than that on which it was my privilege to be placed; and though the state could have been no very favorable one for forming a resolution, I in that hour determined that I should never again sacrifice my capacity of intellectual enjoyment to a drinking usage; and with God's help I was enabled to hold by the determination."

In a certain manufacturing town an employer one Saturday paid to his workmen $700 in crisp new bills that had been secretly marked. On Monday $450 of those identical bills were deposited in the bank by the saloon-keepers. When the fact was made known, the workmen were so startled by it that they helped to make the place a no-license town. The times would not be so "hard" for the workmen if the saloons did not take in so much of their wages. If they would organize a strike against the saloons, they would find the result to be better than an increase of wages, and to include an increase of savings.

How often we might read the following sign over the threshold of a youthful life: "For sale, grand opportunities, for a song;" "golden chances for beer;" "magnificent opportunities exchanged for a little sensual enjoyment;" "for exchange, a beautiful home, devoted wife, lovely children, for drink;" "for sale, cheap, all the magnificent possibilities of a brilliant life, a competence, for one chance in a thousand at the gambling table;" "for exchange, bright prospects, a brilliant outlook, a cultivated intelligence, a college education, a skilled hand, an observant eye, valuable experience, great tact, all exchanged for rum, for a muddled brain, a bewildered intellect, a shattered nervous system, poisoned blood, a diseased body, for fatty degeneration of the heart, for Bright's disease, for a drunkard's liver."

With almost palsied hand, at a temperance meeting, John B. Gough signed the pledge. For six days and nights in a wretched garret, without a mouthful of food, with scarcely a moment's sleep, he fought the fearful battle with appetite. Weak, famished, almost dying, he crawled into the sunlight; but he had conquered the demon which had almost killed him. Gough used to describe the struggles of a man who tried to leave off using tobacco. He threw away what he had, and said that was the end of it; but no, it was only the beginning of it. He would chew camomile, gentian, tooth-picks, but it was of no use. He bought another plug of tobacco and put it in his pocket. He wanted a chew awfully, but he looked at it and said, "You are a *weed,* and I am a *man.* I'll master you if I die for it;" and he did, while carrying it in his pocket daily.

There was an abbot that desired a piece of ground that lay conveniently for him. The owner refused to sell; yet with much persuasion he was contented to let it. The abbot hired it and covenanted only to farm it for one crop. He had his bargain, and sowed it with acorns—a crop that lasted three hundred years. So Satan asks to get possession of our souls by asking us to permit some small sin to enter, some one wrong that seems of no great account. But when once he has entered and planted the seeds and beginnings of evil, he holds his ground.

"Teach self-denial and make its practice pleasurable," says Walter Scott, "and you create for the world a destiny more sublime than ever issued from the brain of the wildest dreamer."

Thomas A. Edison was once asked why he was a total abstainer. He said, "I thought I had a better use for my head."

Byron could write poetry easily, for it was merely indulging his natural propensity; but to curb his temper, soothe his discontent, and control his animal appetites was a very different thing. At all events, it seemed so great to him that he never seriously attempted self-conquest. Let every youth who would not be shipwrecked on life's voyage cultivate this one great virtue, "self-control." There is nothing so important to a youth starting out in life as a thoroughly trained and cultivated will; everything depends upon it. If he has it, he will succeed; if he does not have it, he will fail.

"The first and best of victories," says Plato, "is for a man to conquer himself; to be conquered by himself is, of all things, the most shameful and vile."

"Silence," says Zimmerman, "is the safest response for all the contradiction that arises from impertinence, vulgarity, or envy."

"He is a fool who cannot be angry," says English, "but he is a wise man who will not."

Seneca, one of the greatest of the ancient philosophers, said that "we should every night call ourselves to account. What infirmity have I mastered to-day? what passion opposed? what temptation resisted? what virtue acquired?" and then he follows with the profound truth that "our vices will abate of themselves if they be brought every day to the shrift." If you cannot at first control your anger, learn to control your tongue, which, like fire, is a good servant, but a hard master.

It does no good to get angry. Some sins have a seeming compensation or apology, a present gratification of some sort, but anger has none. A man feels no better for it. It is really a torment, and when the storm of passion has cleared away, it leaves one to see that he has been a fool. And he has made himself a fool in the eyes of others too.

The wife of Socrates, Xanthippe, was a woman of a most fantastical and furious spirit. At one time, having vented all the reproaches upon Socrates her fury could suggest, he went out and sat before the door. His calm and unconcerned behavior but irritated her so much the more; and, in the excess of her rage, she ran upstairs and emptied a vessel upon his head, at which he only laughed and said that "so much thunder must needs produce a shower." Alcibiades, his friend, talking with him about his wife, told him he wondered how he could bear such an everlasting scold in the same house with him. He replied, "I have so accustomed myself to expect it, that it now offends me no more than the noise of carriages in the street."

It is said of Socrates, that whether he was teaching the rules of an exact morality, whether he was answering his corrupt judges, or was receiving sentence of death, or swallowing the poison, he was still the same man; that is to say, calm, quiet, undisturbed, intrepid—in a word, wise to the last.

"It is not enough to have great qualities," says La Rochefoucauld; "we should also have the management of them." No man can call himself educated until every voluntary muscle obeys his will.

"You ask whether it would not be manly to resent a great injury," said Eardley Wilmot; "I answer that it would be manly to resent it, but it would be Godlike to forgive it."

"He who, with strong passions, remains chaste; he who, keenly sensitive, with manly power of indignation in him, can be provoked, and yet restrain himself and forgive—these are strong men, the spiritual heroes."

To feel provoked or exasperated at a trifle, when the nerves are exhausted, is, perhaps, natural to us in our imperfect state. But why put into the shape of speech the annoyance which, once uttered, is remembered; which may burn like a blistering wound, or rankle like a poisoned arrow? If a child be crying or a friend capricious, or a servant unreasonable, be careful what you say. Do not speak while you feel the impulse of anger, for you will be almost certain to say too much, to say more than your cooler judgment will approve, and to speak in a way that you will regret. Be silent until the "sweet by and by," when you will be calm, rested, and self-controlled.

But self-respect must be accompanied by self-conquest, or our strong feelings may prove but runaway horses. He who would command others must first learn to obey, and he who would command his own powers must learn to be submissive to the still small voice within. Discipline the passions, curb pride and impatience, restrain all hasty impulses. Deny yourself the gratification of any desire not sanctioned by reason. Shame and its consequent degradation follow the loss of our own good opinion rather than the esteem of others. Too many yield in the perpetual conflict between temptation to gratify the coarser appetites and aspiration for the good, the true, and the beautiful. Voices unheard by those around us whisper "Don't," but too often self-respect is lost, the will lies prostrate, and the debauch goes on. Such battles must be fought by all; be ours the victory born of self-control, aided by that Heaven which always helps him who prays while putting his own shoulder to the wheel.

No man had a better heart or more thoroughly hated oppression than Edmund Burke. He possessed neither experience in affairs, nor a tranquil judgment, nor the rule over his own spirit, so that his genius, under the impulse of his bewildering passions, wrought much evil to his country and to Europe, even while he rendered noble service to the cause of commercial freedom, to Ireland, and to America.

Burns could not resist the temptation to utter his clever sarcasms at another's expense, and one of his biographers has said that he made a hundred enemies for every ten jokes he made. But Burns could no more control his appetite than his tongue.

"Thus thoughtless follies laid him lowAnd stained his name."

Xanthus, the philosopher, told his servant that on the morrow he was going to have some friends to dine, and asked him to get the best thing he could find in the market. Thephilosopher and his guests sat down the next day at the table. They had nothing but tongue—four or five courses of tongue—tongue cooked in this way, and tongue cooked in that way, and the philosopher lost his patience, and said to his servant, "Didn't I tell you to get the best thing in the market?" He said, "I did get the best thing in the market. Isn't the tongue the organ of sociality, the organ of eloquence, the organ of kindness, the organ of worship?" Then Xanthus said, "To-morrow I want you to get the worst thing in the market." And on the morrow the philosopher sat at the table, and there was nothing there but tongue—four or five courses of tongue—tongue in this shape, and tongue in that shape—and the philosopher again lost his patience, and said, "Didn't I tell you to get the worst thing in the market?" The servant replied, "I did; for isn't the tongue the organ of blasphemy, the organ of defamation, the organ of lying?"

"I can reform my people," said Peter the Great, "but I cannot reform myself." He forbade all Russians to wear beards, and to quell the insurrection which resulted, he had 8000 revolters beheaded. With a hatchet he began the ghastly work. He had his own son beheaded.

He who cannot resist temptation is not a man. He is wanting in the highest attributes of humanity. The honor and nobleness of the old "knight-errantry" consisted in defending the innocence of men and protecting the chastity of women against the assaults of others. But the truer and nobler knighthood protects the property and the character, the innocence and the chastity of others against one's self. We should all be posted upon our weak points, for after all there are many emergencies in life when these weak points, not our strong ones, will measure our manhood and our strength. Many a woman whom a mouse would frighten out of her wits would not shrink from assisting in terrible surgical operations in our city or war hospitals, and many an officer and soldier who would walk up to the cannon's mouth without a tremor in battle, would not dare to say his soul was his own in a society parlor. Many a great statesman has quailed before the ringer of scorn of a fellow-Congressman, and has been completely cowed by a hiss from the gallery or a ridiculing paragraph in a newspaper. We all have tender spots, weak spots, and a man can never know his strength who does not study his weaknesses.

"Violent passions and ardent feelings are seldom found united with complete self-command; but when they are they form the strongest possible character, for there is all the power of clear thought and cool judgment impelled by the resistless energy of feeling. This combination Washington possessed; for in his impetuosity there was no foolish rashness, and in his passion no injustice. Besides, whatever violence there might be within, the explosion seldom came to the surface, and when it did it was arrested at once by the stern mandate of his will. He never lost the mastery of himself in any emergency, and in 'ruling his spirit' showed himself greater than in 'taking a city.'

"It is one of the astonishing things in his life that, amid the perfect chaos of feeling into which he was thrown,—amid the distracted counsels and still more distracted affairs that surrounded him,—he never once lost the perfect equilibrium of his own mind. The contagion of fear and doubt and despair could not touch him. He did not seem susceptible to the common influences which affect men. His soul poised on its own centre, reposed calmly there through all the storms that beat for seven years on his noble breast. The ingratitude and folly of those who should have been his allies, the insults of his foes, and the frowns of fortune never provoked him into a rash act, or deluded him into a single error."

Horace Mann says that there must be a time when the vista of the future, with all its possibilities of glory and of shame, first opens to the vision of youth. Then is he summoned to make his choice between truth and treachery; between honor and dishonor; between purity and profligacy; between moral life and moral death. And as he doubts or balances between the heavenward or hellward course; as he struggles to rise or consents to fall; is there in all the universe of God a spectacle of higher exultation or of deeper pathos? Within him are the appetites of a brute and the attributes of an angel; and when these meet in council to make up the roll of his destiny and seal his fate, shall the beast hound out the seraph? Shall the young man, now conscious of the largeness of his sphere and of the sovereignty of his choice, wed the low ambitions of the world, and seek, with their emptiness, to fill his immortal desires? Because he has a few animal wants that must be supplied, shall he become all animal,—an epicure and an inebriate,—and blasphemously make it the first doctrine of his catechism,—"the Chief End of Man?"—to glorify his stomach and enjoy it? Because it is the law of self-preservation that he shall provide for himself, and the law of religion that he shall provide for his family, when he has one, must he, therefore, cut away all the bonds of humanity that bind him to his race, forswear charity, crush down every prompting of benevolence, and if he can have the palace and equipage of the prince, and the table of a sybarite, become a blind man, and a deaf man, and a dumb man, when he walks the streets where hunger moans and nakedness shivers?

The strong man is the one who ever keeps himself under strict discipline, who never once allows the lower to usurp the place of the higher in him; who makes his passions his servants and never allows them to be his master; who is ever led by his mind and not by his inclinations. He drills and disciplines his desires and keeps the roots of his life under ground, and never allows them to interfere with his character. He is never the slave of his inclinations, nor the sport of impulse. He is the commander of himself and heads his ship due north even in the wildest tempests of passion. He is never the slave of his strongest desire.

A noted teacher has said that the propensities and habits are as teachable as Latin and Greek, while they are infinitely more essential to happiness. We are very largely the creatures of our wills. By constantly looking on the bright side of things, by viewing everything hopefully, by setting the face as a flint every hour of every day toward all that is harmonious and beautiful in life, and refusing to listen to the discord or to look at the ugly side of life, by constantly directing the thought toward what is noble, grand and true, we can soon form habits which will develop into a beautiful character, a harmonious and well-rounded life. We are creatures of habit, and by knowing the laws of its formation we can, in a little while, build up a network of habit about us, which will protect us from most of the ugly, selfish and degrading things of life. In fact, the only real happiness and unalloyed satisfaction we get out of life, is the product of self-control. It is the great guardian of all the virtues, without which none of them is safe. It is the sentinel, which stands on guard at the door of life, to admit friends and exclude enemies.

"I call that mind free," says Channing, "which jealously guards its intellectual rights and powers, which calls no man master, which does not content itself with a passive or hereditary faith, which opens itself to light whencesoever it may come, which receives new truth as an angel from heaven, which, whilst consulting others, inquires still more of the oracle within; itself, and uses instructions from abroad, not to supersede, but to quicken and exalt its own energies. I call that mind free which is not passively framed by outward circumstances, which is not swept away by the torrent of events, which is not the creature of accidental impulse, but which bends events to its own improvement, and acts from an inward spring, from immutable principles which it has deliberately espoused. I call that mind free which protects itself against the usurpations of society, which does not cower to human opinion, which feels itself accountable to a higher tribunal than man's, which respects a higher law than fashion, which respects itself too much to be the slave or tool of the many or the few. I call that mind free which through confidence in God and in the power of virtue has cast off all fear but that of wrong-doing, which no menace or peril can enthrall, which is calm in the midst of tumults, and possesses itself though all else be lost. I call that mind free which resists the bondage of habit, which does not mechanically repeat itself and copy the past, which does not live on its old virtues, which does not enslave itself to precise rules, but which forgets what is behind, listens for new and higher monitions of conscience, and rejoices to pour itself forth in fresh and higher exertions. I call that mind free which is jealous of its own freedom, which guards itself from being merged in others, which guards its empire over itself as nobler than the empire of the world."

CHAPTER XVII

STICK

Patience is the courage of the conqueror; it is the virtue, *par excellence*, of Man against Destiny, of the One against the World, and of the Soul against Matter. Therefore this is the courage of the Gospel; and its importance, in a social view—its importance to races and institutions—cannot be too earnestly inculcated.—BULWER.

Perpetual pushing and assurance put a difficulty out of countenance, and make a seeming impossibility give way.—JEREMY COLLIER.

To bear is to conquer fate.—CAMPBELL.

The nerve that never relaxes, the eye that never blenches, the thought that never wanders,—these are the masters of victory.—BURKE.

Let us, then, be up and doing,With a heart for any fate;Still achieving, still pursuing,Learn to labor and to wait.—LONGFELLOW.

"How long did it take you to learn to play?" asked a young man of Geradini. "Twelve hours a day for twenty years," replied the great violinist. Layman Beecher's father, when asked how long it took him to write his celebrated sermon on the "Government of God," replied, "About forty years."

"If you will study a year I will teach you to sing well," said an Italian music teacher to a pupil who wished to know what can be hoped for with study; "if two years, you may excel. If you will practice the scale constantly for three years, I will make you the best tenor in Italy; if for four years, you may have the world at your feet."

Perceiving that Caffarelli had a fine tenor voice and unusual talent, a teacher offered to give him a thorough musical education free of charge, provided the pupil would promise never to complain of the course of instruction given. The first year the master gave nothing but the scales, compelling the youth to practice them over and over again. The second year it was the same, the third, and the fourth, the conditions of the bargain being the only reply to any question in relation to a change from such monotonous drill. The fifth year the teacher introduced chromatics and thorough bass, and, at its close, when Caffarelli looked for something more brilliant and interesting, the master said: "Go, my son, I can teach you nothing more. You are the first singer of Italy and of the world." The *mastery* of scales and diatonics gave him power to sing anything.

"Keep at the helm," said President Porter; "steer your own ship, and remember that the great art of commanding is to take a fair share of the work.

Strike out. Assume your own position. Put potatoes in a cart, over a rough road, and the small ones go to the bottom."

"Never depend upon your genius," said John Ruskin, in the words of Joshua Reynolds; "if you have talent, industry will improve it; if you have none, industry will supply the deficiency."

"The only merit to which I lay claim," said Hugh Miller, "is that of patient research—a merit in which whoever wills may rival or surpass me; and this humble faculty of patience when rightly developed may lead to more extraordinary development of ideas than even genius itself."

Titian, the greatest master of color the world has seen, used to say: "White, red and black, these are all the colors that a painter needs, but he must know how to use them." It took fifty years of constant, hard practice to bring him to his full mastery.

"How much grows everywhere if we do but wait!" exclaims Carlyle. "Not a difficulty but can transfigure itself into a triumph; not even a deformity, but if our own soul have imprinted worth on it, will grow dear to us."

Persistency is characteristic of all men who have accomplished anything great. They may lack in some other particular, have many weaknesses, or eccentricities, but the quality of persistence is never absent in a successful man. No matter what opposition he meets or what discouragements overtake him, he is always persistent. Drudgery cannot disgust him, obstacles cannot discourage him, labor cannot weary him. He will persist, no matter what comes or what goes; it is a part of his nature. He could almost as easily stop breathing.

It is not so much brilliancy of intellect or fertility of resource as persistency of effort, constancy of purpose, that makes a great man. Persistency always gives confidence. Everybody believes in the man who persists. He may meet misfortunes, sorrows and reverses, but everybody believes that he will ultimately triumph because they know there is no keeping him down. "Does he keep at it, is he persistent?" is the question which the world asks of a man.

Even the man with small ability will often succeed if he has the quality of persistence, where a genius without persistence would fail.

"How hard I worked at that tremendous shorthand, and all improvement appertaining to it," said Dickens. "I will only add to what I have already written of my perseverance at this time of my life, and of a patient and continuous energy which then began to be matured within me, and which I know to be the strong point of my character, if it have any strength at all, that there, on looking back, I find the source of my success."

"I am sorry to say that I don't think this is in your line," said Woodfall the reporter, after Sheridan had made his first speech in Parliament. "You had better have stuck to your former pursuits." With head on his hand Sheridan mused for a time, then looked up and said, "It is in me, and it shall come out of me." From the same man came that harangue against Warren Hastings which the orator Fox called the best speech ever made in the House of Commons.

"The man who is perpetually hesitating which of two things he will do first," said William Wirt, "will do neither." The man who resolves, but suffers his resolution to be changed by the first counter-suggestion of a friend—who fluctuates from opinion to opinion, from plan to plan, and veers like a weather-cock to every point of the compass, with every breath of caprice that blows, can never accomplish anything great or useful. Instead of being progressive in anything, he will be at best stationary, and, more probably, retrograde in all.

Great writers have ever been noted for their tenacity of purpose. Their works have not been flung off from minds aglow with genius, but have been elaborated and elaborated into grace and beauty, until every trace of their efforts has been obliterated. Bishop Butler worked twenty years incessantly on his "Analogy," and even then was so dissatisfied that he wanted to burn it. Rousseau says he obtained the ease and grace of his style only by ceaseless inquietude, by endless blotches and erasures. Virgil worked eleven years on the Æneid. The note-books of great men like Hawthorne and Emerson are tell-tales of enormous drudgery, of the years put into a book which may be read in an hour. Montesquieu was twenty-five years writing his "Esprit de Louis," yet you can read it in sixty minutes. Adam Smith spent ten years on his "Wealth of Nations." A rival playwright once laughed at Euripides for spending three days on three lines, when he had written five hundred lines. "But your five hundred lines in three days will be dead and forgotten, while my three lines will live forever," replied Euripides.

Sir Fowell Buxton thought he could do as well as others, if he devoted twice as much time and labor as they did. Ordinary means and extraordinary application have done most of the great things in the world.

Defoe offered the manuscript of Robinson Crusoe to many booksellers and all but one refused it. Addison's first play, Rosamond, was hissed off the stage, but the editor of the Spectator and Tattler was made of stern stuff and was determined that the world should listen to him, and it did.

David Livingstone said: "Those who have never carried a book through the press can form no idea of the amount of toil it involves. The process has increased my respect for authors a thousand-fold. I think I would rather cross the African continent again than undertake to write another book."

"For the statistics of the negro population of South America alone," says Robert Dale Owen, "I examined more than a hundred and fifty volumes."

Another author tells us that he wrote paragraphs and whole pages of his book as many as fifty times.

It is said of one of Longfellow's poems that it was written in four weeks, but that he spent six months in correcting and cutting it down. Bulwer declared that he had rewritten some of his briefer productions as many as eight or nine times before their publication. One of Tennyson's pieces was rewritten fifty times. John Owen was twenty years on his "Commentary on the Epistle to the Hebrews;" Gibbon on his "Decline and Fall," twenty years; and Adam Clark, on his "Commentary," twenty-six years. Carlyle spent fifteen years on his "Frederick the Great."

A great deal of time is consumed in reading before some books are prepared. George Eliot read 1000 books before she wrote "Daniel Deronda." Allison read 2000 before he completed his history. It is said of another that he read 20,000 and wrote only two books.

Virgil spent several years on the Georgics, which could be printed in two columns of an ordinary newspaper.

"Generally speaking," said Sydney Smith, "the life of all truly great men has been a life of intense and incessant labor. They have commonly passed the first half of life in the gross darkness of indigent humility,—overlooked, mistaken, condemned by weaker men,—thinking while others slept, reading while others rioted, feeling something within them that told them they should not always be kept down among the dregs of the world. And then, when their time has come, and some little accident has given them their first occasion, they have burst out into the light and glory of public life, rich with the spoils of time, and mighty in all the labors and struggles of the mind."

Malibran said: "If I neglect my practice a day, I see the difference in my execution; if for two days, my friends see it; and if for a week, all the world knows my failure." Constant, persistent struggle she found to be the price of her marvelous power.

"If I am building a mountain," said Confucius, "and stop before the last basketful of earth is placed on the summit, I have failed."

"Young gentlemen," said Francis Wayland, "remember that nothing can stand day's work."

America will never produce any great art until our resources are developed and we get more time. As a people we have not yet learned the art of patience. We do not know how to wait. Think of an American artist spending seven, eight, ten, and even twelve years on a single painting as did Titian, Michael Angelo and many of the other old masters. Think of an American sculptor spending years and years upon a single masterpiece, as did the Greeks and Romans. We have not yet learned the secret of working and waiting.

"The single element in all the progressive movements of my pencil," said the great David Wilkie, "was persevering industry."

The kind of ability which most men rank highest is that which enables its possessor to do what he undertakes, and attain the object of his ambition or desire.

"The reader of a newspaper does not see the first insertion of an ordinary advertisement," says a French writer. "The second insertion he sees, but does not read; the third insertion he reads; the fourth insertion he looks at the price; the fifth insertion he speaks of it to his wife; the sixth insertion he is ready to purchase, and the seventh insertion he purchases."

The large fees which make us envy the great lawyer or doctor are not remuneration for the few minutes' labor of giving advice, but for the mental stores gathered during the precious spare moments of many a year while others were sleeping or enjoying holidays. A client will frequently object to paying fifty dollars for an opinion written in five minutes, but such an opinion could be written only by one who has read a hundred law books. If the lawyer had not previously read those books, but should keep a client waiting until he could read them with care, there would be fewer complaints that fees of this kind are not earned.

We are told that perseverance built the pyramids on Egypt's plains, erected the gorgeous temple at Jerusalem, inclosed in adamant the Chinese Empire, scaled the stormy, cloud-capped Alps, opened a highway through the watery wilderness of the Atlantic, leveled the forests of the new world, and reared in its stead a community of States and nations. Perseverance has wrought from the marble block the exquisite creations of genius, painted on canvas the gorgeous mimicry of nature, and engraved on a metallic surface the viewless substance of the shadow. Perseverance has put in motion millions of spindles, winged as many flying shuttles, harnessed thousands of iron steeds to as many freighted cars, and sent them flying from town to town and nation to nation; tunneled mountains of granite, and annihilated space with the lightning's speed. Perseverance has whitened the waters of the world with the sails of a hundred nations, navigated every sea and explored every land. Perseverance has reduced nature in her thousand forms to as many sciences, taught her laws, prophesied her future movements, measured her untrodden spaces, counted her myriad hosts of worlds, and computed their distances, dimensions, and velocities.

"Whoever is resolved to excel in painting, or, indeed, in any other art," said Reynolds, "must bring all his mind to bear upon that one object from the moment that he rises till he goes to bed."

"If you work hard two weeks without selling a book," wrote a publisher to an agent, "you will make a success of it."

"Know thy work and do it," said Carlyle; "and work at it like a Hercules. One monster there is in the world—an idle man."

CHAPTER XVIII

SAVE

If you want to test a young man and ascertain whether nature made him for a king or a subject, give him a thousand dollars and see what he will do with it. If he is born to conquer and command, he will put it quietly away till he is ready to use it as opportunity offers. If he is born to serve, he will immediately begin to spend it in gratifying his ruling propensity.—PARTON.

The man who builds, and lacks wherewith to pay,Provides a home from which to run away.—YOUNG.

Buy what thou hast no need of, and ere long thoushalt sell thy necessaries.

For age and want save while you may:No morning sun lasts a whole day.—FRANKLIN.

Whatever be your talents, whatever be your prospects, never speculate away on a chance of a palace that which you may need as a provision against the workhouse.—BULWER.

"What do you do with all these books?" "Oh, that library is my 'one cigar a day,'" was the response. "What do you mean?" "Mean! Just this: when you bothered me so about being a man, and learning to smoke, I'd just been reading about a young fellow who bought books with money that others would have spent in smoke, and I thought I'd try and do the same. You remember, I said I should allow myself one cigar a day." "Yes." "Well, I never smoked. I just put by the price of a five-cent cigar every day, and as the money accumulated I bought books—the books you see there." "Do you mean to say that those books cost no more than that? Why there are dollars' worth of them." "Yes, I know there are. I had six years more of my apprenticeship to serve when you persuaded me to 'be a man.' I put by the money I have told you of, which of course at five cents a day amounted to $18.25 a year or $109.50 in six years. I keep those books by themselves, as a result of my apprenticeship cigar-money; and if you'd done as I did, you would by this time have saved many, many more dollars than that, and been in business besides."

If a man will begin at the age of twenty and lay by twenty-six cents every working day, investing at 7 per cent. compound interest, he will have thirty-two thousand dollars when he is seventy years old. Twenty cents a day is no unusual expenditure for beer or cigars, yet in fifty years it would easily amount to twenty thousand dollars. Even a saving of one dollar a week from the date of one's majority would give him one thousand dollars for each of the last ten of the allotted years of life. "What maintains one vice would bring up two children."

Who does not feel honored by his relationship to Dr. Franklin, whether as a townsman or a countryman, or even as belonging to the same race? Who does not feel a sort of personal complacency in that frugality of his youth which laid the foundation for so much competence and generosity in his mature age; in that wise discrimination of his outlays, which held the culture of the soul in absolute supremacy over the pleasures of the sense; and in that consummate mastership of the great art of living, which has carried his practical wisdom into every cottage in Christendom, and made his name immortal? And yet, how few there are among us who would not disparage, nay, ridicule and contemn a young man who should follow Franklin's example.

Washington examined the minutest expenditures of his family, even when President of the United States. He understood that without economy none can be rich, and with it none need be poor.

Napoleon examined his domestic bills himself, detected overcharges and errors.

Unfortunately Congress can pass no law that will remedy the vice of living beyond one's means.

"We are ruined," says Colton, "not by what we really want, but by what we think we do. Therefore never go abroad in search of your wants; if they be real wants, they will come home in search of you; for he that buys what he does not want will soon want what he cannot buy."

"I hope that there will not be another sale," exclaimed Horace Walpole, "for I have not an inch of room nor a farthing left." A woman once bought an old door-plate with "Thompson" on it because she thought it might come in handy some time. The habit of buying what you don't need because it is cheap encourages extravagance. "Many have been ruined by buying good pennyworths."

Barnum tells the story of one of his acquaintances, whose wife would have a new and elegant sofa, which in the end cost him thirty thousand dollars. When the sofa reached the house it was found necessary to get chairs "to match," then sideboards, carpets, and tables, "to correspond" with them, and so on through the entire stock of furniture, when at last it was found that the house itself was quite too small and old-fashioned for the furniture, and a new one was built "to correspond" with the sofa and *et ceteras*: "thus," added my friend, "running up an outlay of $30,000 caused by that single sofa, and saddling on me in the shape of servants, equipage, and the necessary expenses attendant on keeping up a fine 'establishment' a yearly outlay of eleven thousand dollars, and a habit of extravagance which was a constant menace to my prosperity."

Cicero said: "Not to have a mania for buying, is to possess a revenue." Many are carried away by the habit of bargain-buying. "Here's something wonderfully cheap; let's buy it." "Have you any use for it?" "No, not at present; but it is sure to come in useful, some time."

"Annual income," says Macawber, "twenty pounds; annual expenditure, nineteen six, result—happiness. Annual income, twenty pounds; annual expenditure, twenty pounds ought and six, result—misery."

"Hunger, rags, cold, hard work, contempt, suspicion, unjust reproach, are disagreeable," says Horace Greeley; "but debt is infinitely worse than them all."

"If I had but fifty cents a week to live on," said Greeley, "I'd buy a peck of corn and parch it before I'd owe any man a dollar."

To find out uses for the persons or things which are now wasted in life is to be the glorious work of the men of the next generation, and that which will contribute most to their enrichment.

Economizing "in spots" or by freaks is no economy at all; it must be done by management.

Let us learn the meaning of economy. Economy is a high, humane office, a sacrament, when its aim is great; when it is the prudence of simple tastes, when it is practiced for freedom, or love or devotion. Much of the economy we see in houses is of a base origin, and is best kept out of sight. Parched corn eaten to-day that I may have roast fowl for my dinner on Sunday, is a baseness, but parched corn and a house with one apartment, that I may be free of all perturbations, that I may be serene and docile to what the mind shall speak, and girt and road-ready for the lowest mission of knowledge or good will, is frugality for gods and heroes.

Like many other boys P. T. Barnum picked up pennies driving oxen for his father, but unlike many other boys he would invest these earnings in knick-knacks which he would sell to others on every holiday, thus increasing his pennies to dollars.

The eccentric John Randolph once sprang from his seat in the House of Representatives, and exclaimed in his piercing voice, "Mr. Speaker, I have found it." And then, in the stillness which followed this strange outburst, he added, "I have found the Philosopher's stone: it is *Pay as you go.*"

In France, all classes, the men as well as the women, study the economy of cookery and practice it; and there, as many travelers affirm, the people live at one-third the expense of Englishmen or Americans. There they know how to make savory messes out of remnants that others would throw away. There they cook no more for each day than is required for that day. With them the art ranks with the fine arts, and a great cook is as much honored and respected as a sculptor or a painter. The consequence is, as ex-Secretary McCullough thinks, a French village of 1000 inhabitants could be supported luxuriously on the waste of one of our large American hotels, and he believes that the entire population of France could be supported on the food which is literally wasted in the United States. Professor Blot, who resided for some years in the United States, remarks, pathetically, that here, "where the markets rival the best markets of Europe, it is really a pity to live as many do live. There are thousands of families in moderately good circumstances who have never eaten a loaf of really good bread, nor tasted a well-cooked steak, nor sat down to a properly prepared meal."

There are many who think that economy consists in saving cheese parings and candle ends, in cutting off two pence from the laundress' bill, and doing all sorts of little, mean, dirty things. Economy is not meanness. The misfortune is also that this class of persons let their economy apply only in one direction. They fancy they are so wonderfully economical in saving a half-penny, where they ought to spend two-pence, that they think they can afford to squander in other directions. *Punch*, in speaking of this "one idea" class of people, says, "They are like a man who bought a penny herring for his family's dinner, and then hired a coach and four to take it home." I never knew a man to succeed by practicing this kind of economy. True economy consists in always making the income exceed the out-go. Wear the old clothes a little longer, if necessary; dispense with the new pair of gloves, live on plainer food if need be. So that under all circumstances, unless some unforeseen accident occurs, there will be a margin in favor of the income. A penny here and a dollar there placed at interest go on accumulating, and in this way the desired result is obtained.

"I wish I could write all across the sky in letters of gold," says Rev. William Marsh, "the one word, savings bank."

Boston savings banks have $130,000,000 on deposit, mostly saved in driblets. Josiah Quincy used to say that the servant girls built most of the palaces on Beacon street.

"Nature uses a grinding economy," says Emerson, "working up all that is wasted to-day into to-morrow's creation; not a superfluous grain of sand for all the ostentation she makes of expense and public works. She flung us out in her plenty, but we cannot shed a hair or a paring of a nail but instantly she snatches at the shred and appropriates it to her general stock. Last summer's flowers and foliage decayed in autumn only to enrich the earth this year for other forms of beauty. Nature will not even wait for our friends to see us, unless we die at home. The moment the breath has left the body she begins to take us to pieces, that the parts may be used again for other creations."

"So apportion your wants that your means may exceed them," says Bulwer. "With one hundred pounds a year I may need no man's help; I may at least have 'my crust of bread and liberty.' But with £5000 a year I may dread a ring at my bell; I may have my tyrannical master in servants whose wages I cannot pay; my exile may be at the fiat of the first long-suffering man who enters a judgment against me; for the flesh that lies nearest my heart some Shylock may be dusting his scales and whetting his knife. Every man is needy who spends more than he has; no man is needy who spends less. I may so ill manage, that with £5000 a year I purchase the worst evils of poverty—terror and shame; I may so well manage my money, that with £100 a year I purchase the best blessings of wealth: safety and respect."

CHAPTER XIX

LIVE UPWARD

"Do what thou dost as if the stake were heaven,And this thy last deed ere the judgment day."

If you wish to reach the highest begin at the lowest.—PUBLIUS SYRUS.

What is a man,If his chief good, and market of his time,Be but to sleep, and feed? A beast, no more.Sure He, that made us with such large discourse,Looking before, and after, gave us notThat capability and godlike ReasonTo rust in us unused.—SHAKESPEARE.

Ambition is the spur that makes man struggle with destiny. It is heaven's own incentive to make purpose great and achievement greater.—ANONYMOUS.

"Not failure, but low aim, is crime."

"Endeavor to be first in thy calling, whatever itmay be; neither let anyone go before thee in welldoing."

O may I join the choir invisibleOf those immortal dead who live againIn minds made better by their presence; liveIn pulses stirred to generosity,In deeds of daring rectitude, in scornFor miserable aims that end with self,In thoughts sublime that pierce the night like stars,And with their mild persistence urge man's searchTo vaster issues.—GEORGE ELIOT.

"Alexander, Cæsar, Charlemagne and myself have founded empires," said Napo leon to Montholon at St. Helena; "but upon what did we rest the creations of our genius? Upon force. Jesus Christ alone founded his empire on love, and at this moment millions of men would die for Him. I die before my time and my body will be given back to worms. Such is the fate of him who has been called the great Napoleon. What an abyss between my deep misery and the eternal kingdom of Christ, which is proclaimed, loved and adored, and which is extended over the whole earth. Call you this dying? Is it not rather living? The death of Christ is the death of a God."

"No true man can live a half life," says Phillips Brooks, "when he has genuinely learned that it is a half life. The other half, the higher half, must haunt him."

"Ideality," says Horace Mann, "is only the *avant courier* of the mind; and where that in a healthy and normal state goes I hold it to be a prophecy that realization can follow."

"If the certainty of future fame bore Milton rejoicing through his blindness, or cheered Galileo in his dungeon," writes Bulwer, "what stronger and holier support shall not be given to him who has loved mankind as his brothers and devoted his labors to their cause?—who has not sought, but relinquished, his own renown?—who has braved the present censures of men for their future benefit, and trampled upon glory in the energy of benevolence? Will there not be for him something more powerful than fame to comfort his sufferings and to sustain his hopes?"

"If I live," wrote Rufus Choate in his diary in September, 1844, "all blockheads which are shaken at certain mental peculiarities shall know and feel a reasoner, a lawyer and a man of business."

I have read that none of the humbler races have the muscle by which man turns his eye upward, though I am not anatomist enough to be sure of the fact.

"Show me a contented slave," says Burke, "and I will show you a degraded man."

"They truly are faithful," says one writer, "who devote their entire lives to amendment."

General Grant said of the Chinese Wall: "I believe that the labor expended on this wall could have built every railroad in the United States, every canal and highway, and most, if not all, our cities."

"The real benefactors of mankind," says Emerson, "are the men and women who can raise their fellow beings out of the world of corn and money, who make them forget their bank account by interesting them in their higher selves; who can raise mere money-getters into the intellectual realm, where they will cease to measure greatness and happiness by dollars and cents; who can make men forget their stomachs and feast on being's banquet."

"Men are not so much mistaken in desiring to advance themselves," said Beecher, "as in judging what will be an advance, and what the right method of obtaining it. An ambition which has conscience in it will always be a laborious and faithful engineer, and will build the road and bridge the chasms between itself and eminent success by the most faithful and minute performances of duty. The liberty to go higher than we are is given only when we have fulfilled amply the duty of our present sphere. Thus men are to rise upon their performances and not upon their discontent. And this is the secret and golden meaning of the command to be *content* in whatever sphere we are placed. It is not to be the content of indifference, of indolence, of unambitious stupidity, but the content of industrious fidelity. When men are building the foundations of vast structures they must needs labor far below the surface, and in disagreeable conditions. But every course of stone which they lay raises them higher; and at length, when they reach the surface, they have laid such solid work under them that they need not fear now to carry up their walls, through towering stories, till they overlook the whole neighborhood. A man proves himself fit to go higher who shows that he is faithful where he is. A man that will not do well in his present place, because he longs to be higher, is fit neither to be where he is nor yet above it; he is already too high and should be put lower."

Do that which is assigned thee and thou canst not hope too much, or dare too much. What a man does, that he has. In himself is his might. Don't waste life on doubts and fears. Spend yourself on the work before you, well assured that the performance of this hour's duties will be the best preparation for the hours or ages that follow it.

Tradition says that when Solomon received the gift of an emerald vase from the Queen of Sheba he filled it with an elixir which he only knew how to prepare, one drop of which would prolong life indefinitely. A dying criminal begged for a drop of the precious fluid, but Solomon refused to prolong a wicked life. When good men asked for it they were refused, or failed to obtain it when promised, as the king would forget or prefer not to open the vase to get but a single drop. When at last the king became ill, and bade his servants bring the vase, he found that the contents had all evaporated. So it is often with our hope, our faith, our ambition, our aspiration.

A man cannot aspire if he looks down. God has not created us with aspirations and longings for heights to which we cannot climb. Live upward. The unattained still beckons us toward the summit of life's mountains, into the atmosphere where great souls live and breathe and have their being. Even hope is but a promise of the possibility of its own fulfillment. Life should be lived in earnest. It is no idle game, no farce to amuse and be forgotten. It is a stern reality, fuller of duties than the sky of stars. You cannot have too much of that yearning which we call aspiration, for, even though you do not attain your ideal, the efforts you make will bring nothing but blessing; while he who fails of attaining mere worldly goals is too often eaten up with the canker-worm of disappointed ambition. To all will come a time when the love of glory will be seen to be but a splendid delusion, riches empty, rank vain, power dependent, and all outward advantages without inward peace a mere mockery of wretchedness. The wisest men have taken care to uproot selfish ambition from their breasts. Shakespeare considered it so near a vice as to need extenuating circumstances to make it a virtue.

Who has not noticed the power of love in an awkward, crabbed, shiftless, lazy man? He becomes gentle, chaste in language, energetic. Love brings out the poetry in him. It is only an idea, a sentiment, and yet what magic it has wrought. Nothing we can see has touched the man, yet he is entirely transformed.

Not less does ambition completely transform a human being, for a woman thirsting for fame can work where a man equally resolute would faint. He despises ease and sloth, welcomes toil and hardship, and shakes even kingdoms to gratify his master passion. Mere ambition has impelled many a man to a life of eminence and usefulness; its higher manifestation, aspiration, has led him beyond the stars. If the aim be right the life in its details cannot be far wrong. Your heart must inspire what your hands execute, or the work will be poorly done. The hand cannot reach higher than does the heart.

But do not strive to reach impossible goals. It is wholly in your power to develop yourself, but not necessarily so to make yourself a king. How many Presidents of the United States or Prime Ministers of England are chosen within the working lifetime of a man? What if a thousand young men resolve to become President or Prime Minister? While such prizes are within your reach, remember that your will must be tremendous and your qualifications of the highest order, or you cannot hope to secure them. Too many are deluded by ambition beyond their power of attainment, or tortured by aspirations totally disproportionate to their capacity for execution. You may, indeed, confidently hope to become eminent in usefulness and power, but only as you build upon a broad foundation of self-culture; while, as a rule, specialists in ambition as in science are apt to become narrow and one-sided. Darwin was very fond of poetry and music when young, but after devoting his life to science, he was surprised to find Shakespeare tedious. He said that, if he were to live his life again, he would read poetry and hear music every day, so as not to lose the power of appreciating such things.

God asks no man whether he will accept life. That is not the choice. You *must* take it. The only choice is *how*.

"When I found I was black," said Dumas, "I resolved to live as if I were white, and so force men to look below my skin."

In the collection of the Massachusetts Historical Society is a prospectus used by Longfellow in canvassing, on one of the blank leaves of which are the skeleton stanzas of "Excelsior," which he was evidently evolving as he trudged from house to house.

"Disregarding the honors that most men value and looking to the truth," said Plato, "I shall endeavor in reality to live as virtuously as I can; and, when I die, to die so. And I invite all other men to the utmost of my power; and you, too, I invite to this contest, which, I affirm, surpasses all contests here."

"Did you ever hear of a man who had striven all his life faithfully and singly toward an object, and in no measure obtained it?" asked Thoreau. "If a man constantly aspires, is he not elevated? Did ever a man try heroism, magnanimity, truth, sincerity, and find that there was no advantage in them,— that it was a vain endeavor?"

"O if the stone can only have some vision of the temple of which it is to be a part forever," exclaimed Phillips Brooks, "what patience must fill it as it feels the blows of the hammer, and knows that success for it is simply to let itself be wrought into what shape the master wills."

Man never reaches heights above his habitual thought. It is not enough now and then to mount on wings of ecstasy into the infinite. We must habitually dwell there. The great man is he who abides easily on heights to which others rise occasionally and with difficulty. Don't let the maxims of a low prudence daily dinned into your ears lower the tone of your high ambition or check your aspirations. Hope lifts us step by step up the mysterious ladder, the top of which no eye hath ever seen. Though we do not find what hope promised, yet we are stronger for the climbing, and we get a broader outlook upon life which repays the effort. Indeed, if we do not follow where hope beckons, we gradually slide down the ladder in despair. Strive ever to be at the top of your condition. A high standard is absolutely necessary.

www.ingramcontent.com/pod-product-compliance
Lightning Source LLC
Chambersburg PA
CBHW081241220326
41597CB00023BA/4341